Volume 01
Issue 02
July 2006

The Senses & Society

BERG

AIMS AND SCOPE

A heightened interest in the role of the senses in culture and society is sweeping the human sciences, supplanting older paradigms and challenging conventional theories of representation.

This pioneering journal provides a crucial forum for the exploration of this vital new area of inquiry. It brings together groundbreaking work in the humanities and social sciences and incorporates cutting-edge developments in art, design, and architecture. Every volume contains something for and about each of the senses, both singly and in all sorts of novel configurations.

Sensation is fundamental to our experience of the world. Shaped by culture, gender, and class, the senses mediate between mind and body, idea and object, self and environment. The senses are increasingly extended beyond the body through technology, and catered to by designers and marketers, yet persistently elude all efforts to capture and control them. Artists now experiment with the senses in bold new ways, disrupting conventional canons of aesthetics.

- How is perception shaped by cultures and technologies?
- In what ways are the senses sites for the production and practice of ideologies of gender, class, and race?
- How many senses are there to "aesthetics"?
- What are the social implications of the increasing commercialization of sensation?
- How might a focus on the cultural life of the senses yield new insights into processes of cognition and emotion?

The Senses & Society aims to:

- Explore the intersection between culture and the senses
- Promote research on the politics of perception and the aesthetics of everyday life
- Address architectural, marketing, and design initiatives in relation to the senses
- Publish reviews of books and multi-sensory exhibitions throughout the world
- Publish special issues concentrating on particular themes relating to the senses

To submit an article, please write to Michael Bull at:

The Senses and Society
Department of Media & Film Studies
University of Sussex
Brighton
Sussex
BN1 9QQ
UK

email:
senses@sussex.ac.uk or
m.bull@sussex.ac.uk

Books for review should be sent to David Howes at:

The Senses and Society
Department of Sociology and Anthropology
Concordia University
1455 de Maisonneuve Boulevard West
Montreal, Quebec
H3G 1M8
CANADA

email:
senses@alcor.concordia.ca
howesd@vax2.concordia.ca

Comments and suggestions regarding Sensory Design reviews should be addressed to Joy Monice Malnar

email:
malnar@uiuc.edu

Comments and suggestions regarding multisensory exhibition and conference reviews should be addressed to Bill Arning

email:
barning@mit.edu

©2006 Berg. All rights reserved.
No part of this publication may be reproduced or utilized in any form or by any means, electronic or mechanical, including photocopying and recording, or by any information storage or retrieval system, without permission in writing from the publisher.

ISSN: 1745-8927

SUBSCRIPTION INFORMATION

Three issues per volume.

One volume per annum.

2006: Volume 1

ONLINE
www.bergpublishers.com

BY MAIL
Berg Publishers
C/o Customer Services
Turpin Distribution
Pegasus Drive
Stratton Business Park
Biggleswade
Bedfordshire SG18 8TQ
UK

BY FAX
+44 (0)1767 601640

BY TELEPHONE
+44 (0)1767 604951

BY EMAIL
custserv@turpin-distribution.com

INQUIRIES
Kathryn Earle, Managing Editor
email: kearle@bergpublishers.com

Production: Ian Critchley, email:
icritchley@bergpublishers.com

Advertising and subscriptions:
Veruschka Selbach,
email: vselbach@bergpublishers.com

SUBSCRIPTION RATES

Institutions' subscription rate
£155/US$289

Individuals' subscription rate
£40/US$70*

*This price is available only to personal subscribers and must be prepaid by personal cheque or credit card

Free online subscription for institutional subscribers

Full colour images available online

Access your electronic subscription through www.ingenta.com or www.ingentaselect.com

REPRINTS FOR MAILING

Copies of individual articles may be obtained from the publishers at the appropriate fees.
Write to

Berg Publishers
1st Floor, Angel Court
81 St Clements Street
Oxford OX4 1AW
UK

Founding Editors
Michael Bull and David Howes

EDITORIAL BOARD

Managing Editor
Michael Bull, University of Sussex, UK

Editors
Paul Gilroy, London School of Economics, UK

David Howes, Concordia University, Canada

Douglas Kahn, University of California, Davis, USA

Sensory Design Editor
Joy Monice Malnar, University of Illinois, Urbana-Champaign

Book Reviews Editor
David Howes, Concordia University

Exhibition and Conference Reviews Editor
Bill Arning, Massachusetts Institute of Technology, USA

ADVISORY BOARD

Alison Clarke, *University of Vienna, Austria*

Steven Connor, *University of London, UK*

Alain Corbin, *Université de Paris I, La Sorbonne, France*

Ruth Finnegan, *Open University, UK*

Jukka Gronow, *University of Uppsala, Sweden*

Peter Charles Hoffer, *University of Georgia, USA*

Caroline Jones, *Massachusetts Institute of Technology, USA*

Barbara Kirshenblatt-Gimblett, *New York University, USA*

Margaret Morse, *University of California at Santa Cruz, USA*

Ruth Phillips, *Carleton University, Canada*

Leigh Schmidt, *Princeton University, USA*

Mark Smith, *University of South Carolina, USA*

Jonathan Sterne, *McGill University, Canada*

Paul Stoller, *West Chester University, USA*

Michael Syrotinski, *University of Aberdeen, UK*

Nigel Thrift, *University of Oxford, UK*

Fran Tonkiss, *London School of Economics, UK*

Typeset by JS Typesetting Ltd, Porthcawl, Mid Glamorgan
Printed in the UK

The Senses & Society

**Volume 01
Issue 02
July 2006**

Contents

Articles

165 **"It's not about good taste. It's about tastes good": Bourdieu and Campbell's Soup ... and Beyond**
Danielle Gallegos and Alec McHoul

183 **Sensing the Run: The Senses and Distance Running**
John Hockey

203 **See It, Sense It, Save It: Economies of Multisensuality in Contemporary Zoos**
Nils Lindahl Elliot

225 **Seeing with the Hands, Touching with the Eyes: Vision, Touch and the Enlightenment Spatial Imaginary**
Mark Paterson

Sensory Design

245 **Sporting Sensation**
John F. Sherry, Jr.

249 **Mind and Memory: The Blessed Sacrament Chapel, Church of St. Ignatius**
Ruth Coates

255 **Architecture of the Immediate: Steven Holl's Addition to the Cranbrook Institute of Science**
Stephen Temple

259 **Millennium Park, Chicago: A Sensory Delight, Part 2**
    Landmark Destination: Jay Pritzker Pavilion
      Joy Monice Malnar
    Time (and Again): The Lurie Garden
      David L. Hays

Book and Journal Reviews

269 **Mud, Sweat and Tears**
David Winner, *Those Feet: A Sensual History of English Football*
Reviewed by Steve Redhead

273 **Seeing Under the Skin**
Sara Danius, *The Senses of Modernism: Technology, Perception, and Aesthetics*
Reviewed by Anna-Louise Milne

277 **Changing Senses Across Cultures**
Regina Bendix and Donald Brenneis (eds.), "The Senses," *Etnofoor* 18(1)
Reviewed by Judith Okely

Exhibition Reviews

283 **The Urban Sensorium**
"Sense of the City"
Making Sense of the City by Alan Nash
Prière de ne pas toucher by Michael Carroll

"It's not about good taste. It's about tastes good": Bourdieu and Campbell's Soup... and Beyond

Danielle Gallegos and Alec McHoul

Danielle Gallegos is a research fellow in the Centre for Social & Community Research at Murdoch University; she is a dietitian by profession. Alec McHoul is Professor and Head of School (Media Communication & Culture) at Murdoch University. He has published broadly in the field of linguistic sociology.
a.mchoul@murdoch.edu.au

ABSTRACT   We begin with a general discussion of the ways in which the concept of taste has been treated, moving on to what is sometimes taken as a (if not the) controversy in the field. That controversy centers on the apparent differences between socio-political accounts (Bourdieu) and psychological–emotional accounts (Campbell) of taste. What we then show is that the distinction is just that: apparent, on the surface only. What it conceals is a more deep-seated agreement between the two schools about what it is to be a human subject. Here we take our cue from Foucault and Foucault scholarship (Hunter; Rose; Coveney) and make the argument that what appear to be "theories" of taste are, from a pragmatic point of view, in fact rhetorical exercises of the self akin to cookbooks, advertisements and TV cookery shows. This paper, then, problematizes the emergent field of taste studies and presages an approach beyond those predicated on an essentially Kantian version of human being. That approach takes its cue from ethnomethodological insights about techniques of ordinary practical actions and from Hannah Arendt's idea of the disclosure of the self as fundamental to social being.

What is taste? In any discussion in English of the consumption of food as a cultural object, "taste" seems to have a duality of meaning. It firstly refers to bio-sensory manifestations of oral and olfactory sensation in the discernment of sweet, sour, bitter and salt nuances. Secondly, it refers to a socially-linked concept where to have "good taste" is a sign of distinction, and vice versa. This ambiguity perfectly captures (since it derives from) the Kantian dilemma concerning matters of judgment in general: how can individual, sensual, bodily, tasting-events be anchored in publicly-available rules of taste-as-discernment?

"Taste," then, according to one side of the story, tends to gloss the preferences and choices of an individual and is therefore essentially private. Yet the public is never far away, for everyone may, according to the same story, be assumed to choose what tastes and feels good – including willed preferences for the bad. Accordingly, the ideal of good taste (as discernment or distinction) is meant to move beyond the individual, and to be socially binding. It betokens a potentially universal standard – that is, a standard applicable to all members of a given society by contrast, as we shall see, with its "others." This raises the specter of an ideal that every member would ideally follow. Furthermore, this ideal standard would, again ideally, be socially communicable even if it could never be determined precisely and conceptually, as it were, "in the abstract" (Gronow 1997: 91).

Gronow's identification of the duality of taste mirrors that of Kant. Kant makes the distinction between the taste that is *merely* subjective and that which is *universally* subjective. Taste is simultaneously subjective, in that it relates to individual perceptions and universally subjective, in that to rise to the status of the "beautiful" it needs to be communicated and validated with others. Hence:

> The first of these I may call the taste of sense, the second, the taste of reflection: the first laying down judgements merely private, the second, on the other hand, judgements ostensibly of general validity (public), but both alike being aesthetic (not

practical) judgements about an object merely in respect of the bearing of its representation on the feeling of pleasure or displeasure. (Kant 1952: 54)

Kant elaborates on this by suggesting that taste as a sense – that is "taste of the tongue, the palate and the throat " and what may "be agreeable to the eye and ear "– is based on private feeling and is restricted in scope to the individual (1952: 51). In universal subjectivity, or what is generally considered as "good taste," taste is an idea that we communicate and, in so doing, "we believe ourselves to be speaking with a universal voice, and lay claim to the concurrence of every one" (1952: 56). Kant continues:

> The judgement of taste itself does not postulate the agreement of every one (for it is only competent for a logically universal judgement to do this, in that it is able to bring forward reasons); it only imputes this agreement to every one, as an instance of the rule in respect of which it looks for confirmation, not from concepts, but from the concurrence of others. (1952: 56)

Brillat-Savarin (at least on Barthes' reading) replays Kant's hierarchy of taste as the "tiering of taste." Barthes comments on this tiering when he notes that Brillat-Savarin "decomposes the gustatory sensation in time" as:

1. *direct* (when the flavour is still acting on the front of the tongue);
2. *complete* (when the taste moves to the back of the mouth);
3. *reflective* (at the final moment of judgement).

> All the *luxury* of taste is found in this scale; submitting the gustatory sensation to time actually allows it to develop somewhat in the manner of a narrative, or of a language. (Barthes 1985: 61)

Accordingly – that is, because the concept of taste can be so elusive as to offer no concrete empirical research options – there has been intensive speculation over the mechanics of food choice and the taste-acceptability of food from a vast raft of disciplinary perspectives, including the biological, the anthropological, the psychological and the sociological (Rozin 1982; Douglas and Gross 1981; Falconer et al. 1993; Glanz et al. 1990; Mennell 1996; Mennell et al. 1992; McIntosh 1996; Gronow 1997). For all this endeavor, the answer to the food choice question necessarily remains a riddle – there is (and can be) no one correct response and no one correct combination of responses that can best fit either the private or the public version of "taste," let alone the pair as a whole. Despite this, the issue is routinely simplified, as Santich (1996: 18) concludes when posing the question "so why do we eat what we eat?" and answering: "Because that's the way we were born, the way we are – and because we like those flavours." The question, then, remains effectively unresolved *vis-à-vis* what it is that actually determines preferences for some flavors over others. And, as we shall see, there is a very good (almost built-in) reason for this deep unsatisfiability.

Taking another angle and going a little further than Santich's somewhat tautological and commonsensical solution to the problem, Falk (1994: 79) asks: "how can other's food become our food?"; how do we learn to adopt food that we have not been exposed to historically or culturally – "because that's the way we were born"? This question lies at the root of the success of what is sometimes called "ethnic" food, as if there were a food that were not. In this vein, considering distinctions between "our" food and "theirs," Bourdieu and Campbell have both tried to problematize the taste, fashion and pleasure nexus with more subtle responses, and have both effectively anchored the question of taste in a group of related (and more fundamental) concepts. For Bourdieu, these anchoring concepts are ultimately social; for Campbell they are deeply psychological – the two (let alone the combination of the two as the "poles" of taste studies) thereby preserving the Kantian public–private duality, as we shall see.[1]

Bourdieu's thesis centers on his concept of *habitus*:

> The habitus is both the generative principle of objectively classifiable judgements and the system of classification ... of these practices. It is in the relationship between the two capacities which define the habitus, the capacity to produce classifiable practices and works, and the capacity to differentiate and appreciate these practices and products (taste), that the represented social world, i.e., the space of life-styles, is constituted. (Bourdieu 1984: 170)

Here, according to Featherstone (1987: 123), "tastes and lifestyle preferences, which in our society are frequently individualized, are therefore a product of a specific habitus which in turn can be related to the volume of economic and cultural capital possessed...." Hence "the position a particular occupation, age or gender category, class or class fraction occupies can be mapped onto the social space." So, for Bourdieu and those who follow him, taste is ultimately predicated on social class and the affirmation of class boundaries. Food choice is therefore, according to Coveney's (1996: 50) critical summary, about "positioning people in accordance with their class expectations and their collective consciousness, it is therefore what distinguishes one group from another." Bourdieu himself goes on to argue that the manifestation of taste and its use to delineate social groups is more about "distaste." That is, "in matters of taste, more than anywhere else, all determination is negation; and tastes are perhaps first and foremost distastes, disgust provoked by horror or visceral intolerance ('sick-making') of the tastes of others" (Bourdieu 1984: 56). Bourdieu's move is interesting here: confining his answer to the question of taste to the realm of the public–social, he can no longer prioritize the Kantian counter-category of the private–individual. Supplementing this binary (and so also preserving it), then, another crops up confined to the space of sociality: the distinction between "our" taste and our *dis*taste for the tastes of the "other." General social categorization and demarcation, then, precedes and determines any actual, empirical event of what might be called "tasting."[2]

If Bourdieu argues that tastes, culture and pleasure are both class experiences and historically constructed, other theorists – associated with Colin Campbell's position – take the opposite view: that individuals must "discover pleasure for themselves, their aesthetic responses being a matter of *individual psycho-history* rather than class or group membership" (Gabriel and Lang 1995: 113; our emphasis).[3] For Campbell, modern consumption is effectively reducible to modern hedonism and is characterized by a longing for pleasures generated through the psychological activity of day-dreaming. According to Gabriel and Lang's (1995: 104) critical summary of this position, hedonism has moved on from the traditional "hedonism of sensations attached to the senses" to seeking "pleasure not in sensation but in emotion accompanying all kinds of experiences." Campbell's (1987: 77) argument is therefore that:

> pleasure is sought via emotional and not merely sensory stimulation, whilst, secondly, the images which fulfil this function are either imaginatively created or modified by the individual for self-consumption, there being little reliance upon the presence of "real" stimuli.

Campbell (1987: 89) goes on to say that the essential activity of consumption is not about the machinations of selection, purchase and use. Instead, it involves "the imaginative pleasure-seeking to which the product image lends itself, "real" consumption being largely a resultant of this "mentalistic" hedonism." At this point it is perhaps wise to rehearse Gabriel and Lang's caution over Campbell's very singular view of the consumer as pleasure-seeker. Consumption, for them, *is* about selection and purchase of commodities, so that both the domestic consumer and the tourist are more complex than simply one-dimensional hedonists. Gabriel and Lang (1995: 109) put this succinctly: "it would be bizarre to envisage a single mother shopping for her weekly groceries as being lost in a reverie of pleasure."

What emerges, then, from both Bourdieu and Campbell's accounts is a neophilic consumer (and/or tourist) who is on an endless quest for novelty. The quest is either, for Bourdieu, to reinforce class divides and find novelty as social distinction or, for Campbell, to supply experiences not yet encountered, thus making it possible to "project onto [a] product some of that idealized pleasure which [one] has already experienced in day-dreams and which [one] cannot associate with those familiar products currently being consumed" (Campbell 1987: 89). Campbell goes on to argue that the consumer seeks out the novel rather than the familiar because this "enables him to believe that its acquisition and use can supply experiences which he has not so far encountered in reality" (1987: 89). Yet the consumer needs to situate the novel within a framework of the psychologically familiar in order to maximize the pleasures that it can deliver – to be able to day-dream about something requires pre-given knowledges and expectations.

For Bourdieu, apparently by contrast, pleasure emerges as the central theme for the new middle classes, among whom it has metamorphosed from an old morality of duty simpliciter to a new morality of pleasure *as* a duty.

> Thus whereas the old morality of duty, based on the opposition between pleasure and good, induces a generalized suspicion of the "charming and attractive," a fear of pleasure and a relation to the body made up of "reserve," "modesty" and "restraint," and associates every satisfaction of the forbidden impulses with guilt, the new ethical avant-garde urges a morality of pleasure as a duty. This doctrine makes it a failure, a threat to self-esteem not to "have fun." ... Pleasure is not only permitted but demanded, on ethical as much as on scientific grounds. (Bourdieu 1984: 367)[4]

Featherstone furthers this role of the new middle classes whereby the emergence of pleasure as a duty transforms those classes into "cultural intermediaries" with "an interest in searching for new cultural goods, re-discovering old fashion, de-stabilising existing symbolic hierarchies to make the social space more fluid" (Featherstone 1987: 131). This role of cultural intermediary is best exemplified by Appadurai (1988) when he discusses the role of the middle class as taste-makers in the making and remaking of a national cuisine through the medium of cookbooks.

But, at the end of the day, are the "grand theories" of a Bourdieu or a Campbell, any different – *in their pragmatic and technical effect* – from recipe books? Could they be among the recipe books of the modern self? Or, to switch metaphors, even if Bourdieu's and Campbell's soups result in quite distinct tastes, could it still be that they are made from the same basic stock?

On the surface, Bourdieu's position appears as the very antithesis of the Campbell school of thought on taste: social distinctions (rather than emotional and psychological states) appear to underpin questions of taste. Yet, and this is important, the two positions (roughly associable with Campbell and Bourdieu respectively) make the same epistemological shift. Both positions de-emphasize actual, material and sensory cases of *tasting* and ground them in transcendental categories. It hardly matters, at this level, whether those transcendental categories are psycho-emotional (Campbell) or socio-political (Bourdieu). Both, for all their surface differences, preserve a Kantian version of a human subject caught between, on the one hand, empirical–sensory *events* in a material world (as Kant would say, of the flesh) and, on the other, transcendental *conditions* that are the ultimate roots of such events but which are, in themselves, utterly deracinated ideals.[5] Let us further explore this fundamental assumption at the heart of the two seemingly very distinct accounts of taste.

We can summarize this by means of a simple matrix:

	Transcendental conditions		*Empirical events*	*Goal*
Bourdieu:	Social distinction	→	Tasting as "sense"	Novelty (as social difference)
Campbell:	Psychological drive	→	Tasting as "sense"	Novelty (as new pleasures)

What is critically present in both schools, then, is an initial and abiding separation of the human subject into its empirical (sensory) and transcendental (general conditional) components. This is the model of "man" that Foucault, in *The Order of Things* (1972) refers to as the "empirico-transcendental doublet" characteristic of modernity and particularly instantiated in Kantian thinking. This subject is not historically universal; rather it could always have been otherwise. It is not how we fundamentally *are*, but how, as it were, we have been persuaded to become via the manifold techniques of the self increasingly available as modernity has aged. Instead, then, of thinking of the two "philosophies" of taste as pure theories of an ontically given object ("objective" taste), we could come to view them as being much more like techniques of the self in their own right: rhetorical moves that help re-persuade us, re-confirm us in our dual identities as subjects of modernity. That is, they could be viewed as effectively identical (rather than polar-opposite) *ascesēs* (Gr. "training") or practical ethics.[6]

Bourdieu, to be sure, as we have just now seen, mentions the *domain* of the ethical (by and large as an effect of social class). But what he does not see is how his own (along with Campbell's) fundamental view of what it is to be human is an actual instance of a rhetorical technique for producing a particular kind of "ethical subject." These are not "theories" of taste, then, but contributions to technologies of practical subject formation. Here they find themselves ranked with other such technologies of taste as cookery programs on TV, recipe books, advertisements and home economics lessons.

This relocation of what *appear* as theories (but *act* as ethical exercises) points us in a new direction for the analysis of taste – a direction we can barely begin to sketch in this forum. On this view, pleasure becomes part of self-formation as an "ethical subject." Taste and fashion, or as Coveney (1996: 106) describes them "manners and customs," are a part of those pragmatic and historical (or "evental") techniques that are designed to generate pleasures of quite specific kinds:

> Within contemporary Western society conduct around food is problematic, and the pleasures of eating require careful consideration within today's mores, where overt enjoyment of a gustatory nature is invariably modified by manners and customs which are to operate not only in public but also in private.

Here the public–private distinction, so important to the thinking-style of modernity, is considerably loosened. At the level of technique, either "zone" can be effected and acted on identically. Or rather, the distinction between public "good taste" and individual (sensory) tasting is re-valued as a distinction between ethical "sites" corresponding to the two hemispheres of the Kantian self. We find the same rhetorical tropes in, for example, food advertisements in which consumers are not only told a particular food is fashionable (publicly distributed) but also extremely good for an individual to eat and beneficial to their bodily health. In both "high theory" and popular culture, then, we find the same techniques applied to the self by which "individuals come to construe, decipher, act upon themselves in relation to the true and false" (Rose 1992: 144; cf. Foucault 1984, 1985, 1988, 1989). What appears as "true" is any discourse that recognizably and accountably reproduces Western "man" as the empirico-transcendental doublet. Contrastively, what appears as "false" is any discourse that even begins to question this version of the subject as what we fundamentally *are* and always have been – unproblematically.

Taste, then, finally, is an ensemble of (largely rhetorical) techniques for re-affirming a very particular and limited story about ourselves – albeit one that has (because it produces the conditions for) an effective aura of truth. None of the presently available discourses on taste, then, can tell us what it is: for they *must* all count as "true" on our reading. While the present paper has so far problematized this issue, we still await a fully-fledged account that runs radically counter to the currently dominant and very restrictive "true story" of human being and how it tastes.

Can we begin to imagine another account of taste that mobilizes a different and distinct ethics – in which, by "ethics," we refer to any general account of human being, to our ethos? That is, can there be a way of thinking of taste that is at least somewhat beyond what we have so far encountered in Campbell and Bourdieu: a fundamentally Kantian version of "man" as the "empirico-transcendental doublet" (Foucault 1972: 303–43)?

We could start with an utterly sceptical alternative as a working hypothesis. This would run: "taste" is always an abstract concept; it has much the same status as "memory," "love" and "goodness"; to that extent it is properly a matter for metaphysical speculation only; it has no place in the social sciences. Now this would be attractive were it not for its re-singularization of taste – perhaps as a radical response to both Bourdieu and Campbell's dualisms – and were it not for the fact that it would make studies of taste, as concrete consumer practices, impossible. It also neglects the fact that taste can be (though it need not be) a purely physiological matter. So let us see if we can progress from the initial hypothesis to something slightly more workable for practical social-scientific investigation.

The problems with the "ineffability of taste" thesis suggest a further tripartite distinction – which we forward again, to some extent, for the purposes of argument and also knowing that we are still echoing Kant:

1. Taste as physiological fact, e.g. "This food tastes bitter" (Fact).
2. Taste as subjective judgment, e.g. "This food tastes good" (Value A).
3. Taste as public judgment, e.g. "He has good taste in food" (Value B).

Clearly, the social sciences will have little interest in the first two of these; they are the provinces of food science and aesthetics respectively. The third domain, we suggest, is the main locus at which questions of consumption arise and, accordingly, where social scientific interest should be concentrated. But how do we separate the second from the third sense of taste? Both are matters of judgment; both concern the "good."

Wittgenstein in his "Lecture on Ethics" (1965) gives us an initial clue. He makes a division within his well-known logical–ethical, or fact–value, distinction. Within the ethical partition, that is, he distinguishes the relative (ordinary judgment) from the absolute (ethical judgment). Relative propositions include such things as "This is a good football player." Absolute propositions, on the other hand, refer to applications of universal values: "This man's life was valuable" (1965: 6). So when Wittgenstein delimits the *properly* ethical, he is referring to the latter kind of statement, the absolute. Propositions of the first (relative) kind are just ordinary propositions – good football is an empirical matter by and large. But propositions of the second (absolute) kind are instances of what he means by "ethics" as such. They are questions about, for example, what constitutes the value of a life – "the absolute good, the absolute valuable" (1965: 12). And, for Wittgenstein, such questions become hopeless as they move us "beyond significant language" (1965: 11). Ethics proper, as the *Tractatus* has it, is transcendental – it is that whereof we cannot speak (1972: paras 6.421 & 7). Now we have to ask: how do taste domains 2. and 3. (above) map on to this distinction between relative and absolute?

It seems clear that type-2 judgments are relative while type-3s are absolute, at least in Wittgenstein's sense. What I personally find to be *a* good taste (in food or clothing or in any other consumable) is somewhat equal to my judgment that, say, Ryan Giggs is a good footballer. Others may disagree, citing, for example, his merely workmanlike dependability next to an acknowledgedly brilliant improviser like David Beckham. But once good taste *as such* is on the agenda, there is an appeal to a certain absolute set of criteria. One either has it, or one does not. Wittgenstein, however, gives up at this point. We have, he thinks, reached a limit that, if transgressed, will, once again, take us "beyond significant language."

But is this not, itself, a kind of impractical scepticism? Does it not ignore the whole sphere of pragmatics? The "whereof we cannot speak" of absolute ethics is, especially for the early Wittgenstein, in pragmatic terms only a restriction on a certain kind of speaking, a certain kind of discourse. And that kind of discourse is logico-scientific discourse. Wittgenstein's point is that we can't adduce the propositional certainties of natural science in the domain of ethics. So, to put it bluntly, we should realize our limits and shut up once and for all!

Yet logico-scientific discourse is not the only language game at our disposal (and this is what the Wittgenstein of the *Investigations* (1968) realized to have been his fatal mistake in the earlier *Tractatus* (1972).) If we look at the ordinary and quite messy world we inhabit on a day-to-day basis, we find people making all sorts of what the Wittgenstein of the "Lecture" would call absolute judgments: judgments of taste for example. And they do this not as scientific or pseudo-scientific propositions, but in quite different and distinct discourses (or language games). The form of life of science (and its logical reasoning) is not the same as the everyday (and its locally-specific, effective reasoning).

What the early Wittgenstein had forgotten, if we may be so bold, is an important distinction made by Alfred Schütz (1962: 34–47) between first and second order constructs. The natural scientist deals with constructs of the first order: when she arrives on the scene of her investigation, the objects before her are completely open to interpretation. Atoms, galaxies and capybaras have not pre-interpreted themselves. By contrast, human beings are, as the semiotic theorists put it (see Bains (2002)), aware of their capacity to manipulate the sign-relation. They have engaged in manifold and elaborate interpretations of themselves prior to the arrival of the social scientist who is therefore confined to constructs of the second order: interpretations of pre-existing interpretations.

The upshot, for us, of this is that absolute judgments of taste (type-3 versions of taste) are in fact (and routinely) made: but as pragmatic components of the ongoing business of everyday life as self-interpretation. So it may well be the business of taste studies to at least begin to *describe* such things. This would mean a quite different program of studies from those proposed by Bourdieu, Campbell and their ilk.

One way of getting at this domain would be to say that type-3 judgments are routinely narrativized. In the absence of categorical statements about "good taste" (or, for that matter, "bad taste"), human beings are nevertheless able to draw upon multiplicitous stories of their own or others' judgments in order to show (if not strictly to say, propositionally) what they think taste is. For example, in a TV advertisement for Australian beef, some castaways at sea imagine in graphic terms what they *would* like to cook once they have been rescued and returned to their homes. The advertisement runs roughly as follows:

Castaway 1: Well Charles, you're catering officer, what's for dinner tonight?
Castaway 2: Ah. Well. Tonight we have something really special. Steak Parmigiana.
Castaways 1 & 3: Aaah.
Castaway 2: I take a beautifully lean oyster blade steak, seared and sealed on both sides. Then I sauce it lightly in a mixture of onions, basil and white wine. And then, next to it I nestle a scoop of tender macaroni tossed with herbs and alongside that crunchy snow peas. And then, finally, I top off the steak with black olives and melted slices of mozzarella cheese.
Castaway 1: Oooh Charles, you've really excelled yourself this time.
Castaway 3: Best ever!
Their raft bumps into a large ship and a ladder is let down.
Castaway 1: Isn't that always the way, right in the middle of dinner.

Taste is clearly *shown* through this kind of trope, if not stated in so many words. (You read or watch the ad. and you taste at least *something* that may or may not have been actually tasted.) What is happening here is that a taste is made "tellable." To be tellable, something extraordinary has to be envisaged and depicted. Ordinary life as usual is not tellable. Actual practical acts of "tasting" (type-2) have to be fabricated into absolutes (type-3): "Best ever!" As Harvey Sacks reminds us, there is an embargo on the statement of the utterly obvious – we are not obliged, for example, always to answer "truthfully" to the greeting "How are you?" – because it's a greeting not a request for information (Sacks 1975). To put matters of taste (in the type-3 sense) on the agenda is to create an ordinary account of the recognizably – tastably – unobvious, the remark-able, the tell-able.[7] As we said, taste is like memory, love and goodness. To tell you I have a memory of taking a knife from my kitchen drawer this morning to butter my toast is not a legitimate piece of telling. It utterly lacks tellability, for all its truth. To tell you that I took it out of the drawer to stab a burglar is tellable. Ditto for taste. It requires the quotidian

Figure 1
Brown Brothers Advertisement. Courtesy of Brown Brothers Milawa Vineyard Pty Ltd

It's not about good taste. It's about tastes good.

Nothing but the wine.

accounting of something routinely outside the quotidian itself. And it is on these grounds that all forms of consumer culture – from logos and brands to advertising campaigns – depend. The advertisement in Figure 1 puts the matter succinctly – it effectively self-analyses:[8]

This is an example of how we make our own interpretations of our "taste" and our "tastes." This is not "Taste" in any utterly absolute sense. To that extent the early Wittgenstein is right. But for social scientific purposes – for serious investigations of consumer culture – it is what data we have. And each instance can be inspected for a new key to taste and consumption: the locally account-able and practical *fabrication* of the absolute. In the ad., "good taste" (as an absolute) is fabricated as an imaginary foil to something thereby more obviously recognizable: what "tastes good."

To that end, here's a third – though much more famous – fragment of taste "data":

> And then suddenly the memory came to me: it was the taste of a morsel of *madeleine* that my Aunt Léonie used to dip in her tea or in her infusion of lime and give me to sip when I went to her bedroom to say good morning on Sundays.... Before I tasted the little cake that my mother had given me, the sight of it had not reminded me of anything; I had often seen them since the Combray days, displayed in cake-shops, but had never eaten any, which may be why their appearance had become divorced from those days and associated with more recent times. ... (Proust 1982: 34)

This is, of course, Proust recounting how a single moment of tasting a cake is capable of recreating a whole period of "lost time." Here, taste is intimately tied – in a way that sight, for example is not – to another quite specific ethical technique. The presence of the *madeleine* is nothing remarkable for the older Marcel – he has seen many such things before. But now, with the moment of taste, something remarkable (tellable!) does happen: great temporal distances are able to be spanned. Marcel as he was, in his boyhood, becomes completely available to the older man in intimate sensory detail: "the smell and the taste of things, prevailing like disembodied spirits, remembering, waiting, hoping and holding up on their frail but unfaltering foundation the immense edifice of Memory" (1982: 34–5).

Taste, in this case, is a technique for answering an ethical puzzle: how can I still be that totally different person I was then? What is the continuity between moments of the self that leave it, after sufficient time, prone to complete change and difference? Taste acts on *ethical* temporality and difference to fabricate a sense of the self as an historical being. It is in such ways that a public social sense of the self *can be* fabricated in the first place. The self – pace Bourdieu and Campbell – is not easily given by attention to simple formulae such as the reunion of "empirical" and "transcendental" values. Rather it is constantly being made and re-made through, for example, piecemeal ethical techniques of tasting and its remark-ability.

This kind of remark-ability or tellability, then, may be a critical aspect of taste – albeit, as we have seen, one that is neglected in the standard literature on taste. It seems to suggest an ensemble of piecemeal techniques for doing such things as solving ethical puzzles about our very social being whose surface we have only just begun to scratch in this account.

Let us speculate then: that telling our tastes – being unique in *having* our tastes as tellables – is not a mere "nicety" or an option for "chit chat." Rather, it may be part of the very core of our existence as social things: as self-interpreting beings who (alone of all the things we know) have the capacity for self-disclosure. Hannah Arendt puts this as follows – and here she could easily be writing of the disclosure of tastes, though own her concerns are more wide-ranging –

> when I insert myself into the world, it is a world where others are already present. Action and speech are so closely related because the primordial and specifically human act must also answer the question asked of every newcomer: "Who are you?" The disclosure of "who somebody is" is implicit in the fact that speechless action somehow does not exist, or if it exists is irrelevant; without speech [cf. telling], action [cf. tasting] loses the actor, and the doer of deeds is possible only to the extent that he is the speaker of words, who identifies himself as the actor and announces what he is doing. … (2000: 179)[9]

We are not then, as the adage has it, what we consume. Rather we are what it is possible to *dis*-close (open up, un-conceal, tell) of our consuming selves.[10] And this suggests an analysis of taste as the explication of the routine grounds of its telling. Roland Barthes, though in a sense he may not himself have completely recognized, may have been right when he told us earlier that "submitting the gustatory sensation to time" – that is, to time as concrete lived-and-told experience – "actually allows it to develop somewhat in the manner of a narrative, or of a language." The analytic of taste needs to discover some of the basic grammar of that ordinary natural language (pragmatically, from actual cases of its telling and remarking) before it should even dare ponder any grand theory of "Taste" and its necessary reliance on what we have shown to be a very limited idea of human being.

Notes
1. Even the subtitle of Bourdieu's seminal work on taste, *A Social Critique of the Judgement of Taste*, deliberately plays on that of Kant's third critique.
2. Lupton (1996: 35) elaborates on this when she argues that the "revulsion for the food eaten by another is a common expression of discrimination and xenophobia, a means of distinguishing between social groups."
3. Lury (1996: 72) refines this when she argues that Campbell's concept of consumption is self-directed, that there are independent desires to pursue but that this pursuit involves shared cultural values and ideals and does change over time.
4. We will return to this question of ethics below, but in a way that is quite distinct from Bourdieu's own.
5. This summary owes much to Ian Hunter (personal communication).
6. This argument derives from Hunter's (1993) work on Marxism and Romanticism as being less "pure theories" of the human condition and more technical practices for effecting a particular and limited version of it.
7. See Sacks's discussion of *An Ordinary Camp* by Micheline Maurel – an even more extreme case than that of our castaways (1992: 780).
8. It helps to know here that a competing Australian wine producer uses the slogan "Always in good taste."
9. This deep connection between action and talk is remarkably close to that of Harvey Sacks in one of his earliest papers "Sociological Description" (1963) in which he imagines culture as a machine with two parts: the doing and the talking part. Of course, by the end of the paper, the separation is utterly spurious: it cannot be made with any analytic precision. If we want to know, as sociologists do, how people act in the world, we need not describe their actions from a distance, as if they were atoms or electrons; rather we need to find ways of describing *how* they, themselves, tell of (interpret or analyze) their actions – in and as speech-actions in their own

right. There need to be further investigations into the connections between Sacks's and Arendt's (different but related) dis-solutions of the speech/act(ion) distinction and their ramifications for a radically alternative sociology of culture.
10. A further possibility for research is the role played by the crucial Arendtian faculties of "promising" and "forgiving" in telling others about our tastes. Because the upshots of our actions are unknowable in advance, and because our actions are irrevocable once carried out, we have to be able to "promise" (go forward together) and "forgive" (redeem each others' mis-deeds): "forgiving and making promises are like control mechanisms built into the very faculty to start new and unending processes" (2000: 181).

References

Appadurai, Arjun. 1988. "How to Make a National Cuisine: Cookbooks in Contemporary India." *Comparative Studies in Society and History* 30(1): 3–24.

Arendt, Hannah. 2000. "Labor, Work, Action." In P. Baehr (ed.), *The Portable Hannah Arendt*. London: Penguin: 167–81.

Bains, Paul. 2002. "Umwelten." *Semiotica* 134(1/4): 137–67.

Barthes, Roland. 1985. "Reading Brillat-Savarin." In M. Blonsky (ed.), *On Signs*. Oxford: Blackwell: 61–75.

Bourdieu, Pierre. 1984. *Distinction: A Social Critique of the Judgement of Taste*. Translated by R. Nice. London: Routledge and Kegan Paul.

Campbell, Colin. 1987. *The Romantic Ethic and the Spirit of Modern Consumerism*. Oxford: Blackwell.

Coveney, John. 1996. "The Government and Ethics of Nutrition." PhD Diss. Murdoch University.

Douglas, Mary and Jonathan Gross. 1981. "Food and Culture: Measuring the Intricacy of Rule Systems." *Social Science Information* 20(1): 1–35.

Falconer, H. K. Baghurst and E. Rump. 1993. "Nutrient Intakes in Relation to Health-related Aspects of Personality." *Journal of Nutrition Education* 25: 307–19.

Falk, Pasi. 1994. *The Consuming Body*. London: Sage.

Featherstone, Mike. 1987. "Leisure, Symbolic Power and the Life Course." In J. Horne, D. Jary and A. Tomlinson (eds), *Sport, Leisure and Social Relations*. London: Routledge and Kegan Paul: 113–38.

Foucault, Michel. 1972. *The Order of Things: An Archaeology of the Human Sciences*. No trans. named. London: Tavistock.

—— 1984. "On the Genealogy of Ethics: An Overview of Work in Progress." In P. Rabinow (ed.), *The Foucault Reader*. London: Penguin: 340–72.

—— 1985. *The Use of Pleasure: The History of Sexuality Volume Two*. Trans. R. Hurley. London: Penguin.

────── 1988. "The Return of Morality." In L.D. Kritzman (ed.) *Michel Foucault: Politics, Philosophy, Culture*. New York: Routledge: 242–54.

────── 1989. "The Ethic of the Care of the Self as a Practice of Freedom." In J. Bernauer and D. Rasmussen (eds), *The Final Foucault*. Cambridge, MA: MIT Press: 1–20.

Gabriel, Yiannis and Tim Lang. 1995. *The Unmanageable Consumer: Contemporary Consumption and its Fragmentations*. London: Sage.

Glanz, Karen, Frances Marcus Lewis and Barbara K. Rimer. 1990. *Health Behavior and Health Education: Theory, Research and Practice*. San Francisco: Jossey-Bass.

Gronow, Jukka. 1997. *The Sociology of Taste*. London: Routledge.

Hunter, Ian. 1993. "Setting Limits to Culture." In Graeme Turner (ed.) *Nation, Culture, Text: Australian Cultural Studies*. London: Routledge: 140–63.

Kant, Immanuel. [1790] 1952. *Critique of Judgement*. Trans. J. Meredith. Oxford: Oxford University Press.

Lupton, Deborah. 1996. *Food, the Body and the Self*. London: Sage.

Lury, Celia. 1996. *Consumer Culture*. Cambridge: Polity Press.

Maurel, Micheline. 1958. *An Ordinary Camp*. Trans. M. Summers. New York: Simon and Schuster.

McIntosh, William Alex. 1996. *Sociologies of Food and Nutrition*. New York: Plenum Press.

Mennell, Stephen. 1996. *All Manners of Food: Eating and Taste in England and France from the Middle Ages to the Present*. Oxford: Blackwell.

Mennell, Stephen, Anne Murcott and Anneke Otterloo. 1992. *The Sociology of Food: Eating, Diet and Culture*. London: Sage.

Proust, Marcel. [1913-27] 1982. *A Search for Lost Time*. Trans. James Grieve. Canberra: Australian National University Press.

Rose, Nikolas. 1992. "Governing the Enterprising Self." In P. Heelas and P. Morris (eds), *The Values of the Enterprise Culture: The Moral Debate*. London: Routledge: 141–64.

Rozin, Paul. 1982. "Human Food Selection: The Interaction of Biology, Culture and Individual Experience." In L. M. Barker (ed.), *The Psychobiology of Human Food Selection*. Westport, CT: AVI Publishing: 225–53.

Sacks, Harvey. 1963. "Sociological Description." *Berkeley Journal of Sociology* 8: 1–16.

────── 1975. "Everyone Has To Lie." In M. Sanches and B. Blount (eds), *Sociocultural Dimensions of Language Use*. New York: Academic Press: 57–79.

────── 1992. *Lectures on Conversation, Vol. 1*. Edited by G. Jefferson. Oxford: Blackwell, 1992.

Santich, Barbara. 1996. *Looking for Flavour*. Adelaide: Wakefield Press.

Schütz, Alfred. 1962. *Collected Papers Vol. 1: The Problem of Social Reality.* Edited and with an Introduction by M. Natanson. The Hague: Martinus Nijhoff.

Wittgenstein, Ludwig. 1965. "Wittgenstein's Lecture on Ethics." *Philosophical Review* 74: 3–12.

—— 1968. *Philosophical Investigations.* Trans. G.E.M. Anscombe. Oxford: Blackwell.

—— 1972. *Tractatus Logico-Philosophicus.* Trans. D.F. Pears and B.F. McGuinness. London: Routledge and Kegan Paul.

Textile

The Journal of Cloth and Culture

Edited by Pennina Barnett, Goldsmiths College, University of London.
Doran Ross, UCLA Fowler Museum of Cultural History, Los Angeles.

Winner of the 2005 ALPSP/ Charlesworth Award for Best New Journal

'This journal has a lot going for it. It is easy to handle, well printed on good paper, imaginatively designed. Any university or college with an interest in textiles should subscribe to it and make it easily available. For individual scholars and makers, the journal provides a useful resource and will be a pleasure to collect and possess.'

Times Higher Education

Bringing together research in textiles in an innovative and distinctive academic forum, Textile provides a platform for points of departure between art and craft; gender and identity; cloth, body and architecture; labour and technology, techno-design and practice.

Heavily illustrated, Full colour

TEXTILE	
ISSN 1475 9756	
Individual Subscription	
Print only, does not include online access.	£46 / $79
Institutional Print and Online	
Includes online access to all *Textile* back issues.	
Available through www.ingentaconnect.com	£125 / $225

Indexed by:
H.W. Wilson, Ebsco, IBSS (International Bibliography of Social Sciences), DAAI (Design and Applied Arts Index).

Published 3 times a year in March, July and November.

BERG

Order online at www.bergpublishers.com or call +44(0)1767 604951
Institutional subscriptions include online access through www.IngentaConnect.com
To order a sample copy please contact enquiry@bergpublishers.com
View issue 1.1 free online at www.ingentaconnect.com

Sensing the Run: The Senses and Distance Running

John Hockey

John Hockey is a Research Fellow at the University of Gloucestershire who has previously published research in the sociology of occupations, sociology of sport and doctoral education.
jhockey@glos.ac.uk

ABSTRACT To date, there has been little research into the sensuous dimensions of sporting activity. This paper seeks to address this lacuna and to expand the literature via an examination of one specific group: distance runners. Using data from a two-year collaborative autoethnography, the paper portrays the sensuous activity experienced by two runners as they traverse their routine training routes.

Introduction

When surveying the literature on attempts to explain sport at a phenomenological level, Kerry and Armour (2000) found, perhaps surprisingly, a paucity of material. The same state of affairs, with a few exceptions (Kew 1986; Coates 1999) is to be found within ethnomethodology. This paper contributes to the small but growing amount of embodied analysis on the body and sport (Lewis 2000; Rotella 2002; Wacquant 2004; Downey 2005) by analytically portraying something of the corporeal skills, knowledge and experiences of distance runners as they traverse their training routes.[1] The vast majority of running undertaken by these athletes is done during training runs, which far outweighs their involvement in racing. To achieve its objective the paper focuses upon the sensuous experiences (Rodaway 1994) of this sporting practice. It constitutes a response to Classen's (1997: 410) call for "in-depth" investigations of particular sensory phenomena. The paper examines the sensory practices of this routine activity by making use of autoethnographic data.

Autoethnographic Data and Analysis

While autoethnography has its critics (Coffey 1999) it also has a growing number of proponents within sociology and anthropology who have developed powerful justifications for its use (Allen Collinson and Hockey, 2005). It emphasizes the linkage between themes within the author's experience and broader cultural and subcultural processes. For the author and his co-researcher who wished to portray the relationship between the distance running "mind" (emotions, sensations, knowledge) and its embodied activity, it constituted the best means of accessing and depicting that relationship.

In order for the events to be described to be understood in context, it will be necessary first for me to make visible some "accountable" knowledge in terms of athletic biographies. My female training partner/co-researcher and I both have a background of distance running that ranges over five-mile races to marathons and run together habitually. This has required a commitment to training six or seven days a week, on occasion twice a day, for nineteen years and thirty-eight years respectively. Moreover, we have been training together for the past eighteen years. During the same wind-swept week we both suffered knee injuries occasioned by having to train in the winter dark. It was apparent at the onset of these injuries that they did not constitute the usual small niggles that plague the habitual runner. Consequently, we rapidly arrived at a mutual decision to document our response to these injuries systematically, our principal motive being to achieve something positive out of a negative experience. The process of injury and recovery and its documentation took a full two years (Allen Collinson & Hockey 2001; Allen Collinson 2005; Hockey 2005).

Runners habitually keep logs of their daily training performance so the discipline of daily recording information was already *in situ*. Rather than training logs we constructed logs on the process of injury–rehabilitation so as to document our mutual and individual endeavors to return to the status of fully functioning athletes. Both of us constructed a personal log (indicated at the end of the extracts from field notes as Log 1 or Log 2 respectively) that was individually and jointly interrogated for emerging themes using a form of the constant comparative method (Glaser and Strauss 1967). We then created a third, collaborative log made up of these joint themes.

Micro tape recorders constituted the daily means of recording our experiences, and recordings were transcribed and the collaborative log constructed within a day or two of events occurring.

A by-product of our data analysis was that we became aware of a "stock of knowledge" (Benson and Hughes 1983: 52) that we had previously taken for granted when running. The documentation of this was then added to our initial main analytical task, that of recording our response to being injured.

What follows is part of that distance-running stock of knowledge; attempts have been made to made to portray the data evocatively (Denison and Rinehart 2000), so as to provide the reader with something of the sensations of distance running. For example, the sections on how runners see and touch their routes are written as if one of us is running the route, whereas in reality the data on which it is based come from a shared resource both experiential and as a sociological record. So the "I" in the narrative and the narrative itself is a composite of both our collective knowledge of a particular training route and of our documentation of it. Other parts of the data are highlighted in italics, and use is also made of prolonged emphasis on particular words.

Theorizing Training Routes and the Running Body

Theoretically it is possible to categorize these training routes as a particular kind of "social space" (Lefebvre 1991). It is via the embodied activity of training that this particular kind of space is produced or created (Lefebvre 1991; Stewart 1995). In Lefebvre's (1991) terms, we actually engage with our running in a social space that can be fruitfully examined in a number of distinct analytical ways. The first kind of engagement is that of "socially specific spatial practices" (Stewart 1995: 611), which involves the actual physical running through streets and parks that simultaneously creates the particular social space(s) known to us as training routes. The second kind of engagement involves what Lefebvre calls *representations of space*, which are *conceived* spaces. Thus, our routes are also imaginatively constructed via our thoughts, ideas, narratives and memories, as particular kinds of spaces. The combination of these two forms of engagement produce what Lefebvre calls *spaces of representation* or *lived space*. This lived space then produces specific forms of cognitive and corporeal knowing that are the outcomes of spatial practices. These are socially specific in terms of being linked to particular geographical features but also have their own history (Stewart 1995).

Social interaction permeates the lived space of each route and is manifest in two forms, contrary to fictionalized depictions of distance running as being pervaded by loneliness (Sillitoe 1993). Firstly, when runners train together it constitutes a complex interactional accomplishment in terms of maintaining physical proximity over particular stretches of space, which are liable to be variable in terms

John Hockey

Installation view of the CCA exhibition *Sense of the City* © Centre Canadien d'Architecture/Canadian Centre for Architecture, Montréal.
Photo Michel Legendre

of terrain, population, climatic conditions and different levels of ability (fitness, agility, current "form" etc) . Training together, like walking together (Ryave and Schenkein 1975), then, demands of runners considerable interactional work. Aural work involves listening to the breathing pattern and utterances (cursing) of training partners to assess their degree of form. Visual work occurs via "the glance" (Sudnow 1972) as facial expressions and bodily posture are similarly scrutinised for indications of how partners are "going" in any particular session. Further visual work is involved in monitoring the particular path partners are taking so as to avoid collision (Ryave and Schenkein 1975). On the basis of such evaluation synchrony of running performance is achieved via mutual anticipation and interpretation. Secondly, social interaction occurs en route with two categories of public. There is the general public, who are mainly viewed as having the potential to disrupt training routines in terms of impairing performance levels or inflicting injury, either accidentally or on purpose; generally runners develop strategies of avoidance when dealing with this public (Smith 1997). In addition to interaction with the general public there is more positive interaction with individuals who have been encountered en route over prolonged periods, and are identified as being "serious runners" (Smith 1998). The result being the routine exchange of greetings, gestures and the occasional brief conversation about running (Hockey 2005).

In theorizing about the sensual running body the work of Merleau-Ponty is of considerable relevance . For his mission was to reveal "underneath the objective and detached knowledge of the body that other knowledge which we have of it by virtue of its always being with us and of the fact that we are our body" (1962: 206). From this standpoint the body is not so much an instrument nor an object but rather the *subject* of perception. Moreover, for Merleau-Ponty this perception is inextricably linked to movement, and all bodily movement is accompanied by intentionality, which is at the core of perception (1962: 110–11). Social life generally demands habituated bodily action (e.g. driving a car), which becomes taken for granted in a pre-reflective sense. Crossley (2001: 123) neatly sums up Merleau-Ponty's position: "The corporeal schema is an incorporated bodily know-how and practical sense; a perspectival grasp upon the world from the 'point of view' of the body." This practical *sense* is built or developed by habit, but habit for Merleau-Ponty is not a mechanical phenomenon. Rather it is, as Crossley (2001: 127) notes, a practical "principle" that emerges into the social world via the formulation of meaning, intention and appropriate action.

So distance runners have an understanding of how to do distance running, but this understanding is not just cognitive but also corporeal, built by the body immersing itself in habitual training practices. As Crossley (1995: 47) has observed, the mind is inseparable from the body; they remain "reversible aspects of a single fabric." This combination of corporeal and cognitive interacts with a particular physical environment to create a particular form of "emplacement" (Howes 2005: 7). The data will demonstrate how runners move over, listen to, smell, see and feel their training routes. These senses are presented separately for analytic purposes whereas in reality they mutually influence each other (Howes 2003: 47).

Moving En Route

The paper now turns to this physical process of movement that allows athletes to cover their training terrain and produce optimal performances. Given that runners perceive their environment from a moving vantage point, as Ingold (2000: 166) points out, "[l]ocomotion not cognition must be the starting point for the study of perceptual activity." When humans run, the vestibular organs organize the equilibrium of the body dealing with the forces of gravity and their direction (Gibson 1966), so that balance is maintained and locomotion is achieved. The forward movement of running has two principal interrelated components: rhythm and timing. Goodridge (1999: 43) defines rhythm in human physical performance as a "patterned energy-flow of action, marked in the body by varied stress and directional change; also marked by changes in the level of intensity, speed and duration." Rhythm then organizes or shapes the flow of action, while simultaneously being part of that action. There is a general rhythm to doing every distance-running session, and also, within each session the rhythm will change according to how individuals are feeling, the changing terrain and weather. The rhythms of distance running are predominantly cyclical and rooted in the combination of synchronized breathing patterns and lower limb cadence. Moreover, their form is relatively constant when compared to other sports such as soccer, which is characterized by a more intermittent, stop–start form. Achieving rhythm involves, above all, a coordination of bodily parts as the demands of terrain are negotiated via precise bodily adjustments necessary for the chosen footfall and cadence. To do this effectively requires the development of a particular sense of timing. This Goodridge (1999: 44) defines as: "the act of determining or regulating the order of occurrence of an action or event, to achieve desired results." Running demands a particular kind of embodied timing and the performance of distance running and racing requires a specific variant of this.

This was most apparent during the injury and recovery process of the author and his co-runner/researcher: the two-year period involved a loss and subsequent regaining of a particular kind of timing. Our acute sense of timing had been fractured by protracted injury time. For ten months we were unable even to jog and in that time the grounded, embodied understanding of how to run had been lost, as portrayed in the following fieldnote:

> Initially tried some tiny 10-meter trots with rests in between, but to our consternation are like babies! Like drunks we stagger all over the place. No coordination, legs out of kilter with arms, unused to the effort so breathing is *ragged,* legs do not seem to *fit* with the torso, and head feels *wobbly* and *heavy*. Even these baby trots *empty* us, compounding the problem ... (Individual Log 1)

Over a period of fourteen months, we gradually learnt again how to distance run. This necessitated educating ourselves once more in how to coordinate the bodies parts and how to synthesize physiological and cognitive elements in order to build a running rhythm. As the health of our knees gradually improved, our sense of athletic timing gradually came back. Previously, when healthy, this athletic temporal sense had been acute. Either of us could, with some precision, identify the pace of our running, using a spectrum of bodily indicators such as respiratory rate and leg cadence. This timing had been routinely articulated during our training runs. Our sense of timing had been developed and refined by thousands of miles and hours of running practice. As a result of prolonged injury time, our embodied timing had been forgotten. Happily, towards the end of the two years of rehabilitation this sense of timing eventually began to return:

> Going well today, and for the first time I acted like a real runner again. I suddenly said to J: "This *feels* like 7s" (7 minutes per mile), and he nodded agreement... Once finished, I checked on the watch and it was indeed approximately the pace I had felt intuitively. That's a big marker for us – on the way back! (Individual Log 2)

Part of this embodied sense of rhythm and timing is made up of a highly developed awareness of sensations emanating from moving muscles, tendons, ligaments, skin and organs. As Leder (1990: 23) notes, the "body is always a field of immediately lived sensation... Its presence is fleshed out by a ceaseless stream of kinesthesias, cutaneous and visceral sensations..." These sensations provide the individual with information about the choices she/he is making about position, balance and pace: how to stride up- or downhill, how to do "speed work" or to run at a certain pace per mile becomes known via differing assemblages of corporeal sensations that become taken for granted with experience. The angle of the head and torso, placing of the feet, stride length, arm movement and cadence, these constitute the "specific gestures and postures" (Feher 1987: 159) of the distance-running body that are produced via corporeal choices made on the basis of such kinesthetic information. Again, one way of revealing these sensory packages is to depict something of the process of re-learning how to distance run, necessitated by the injury–rehabilitation process previously mentioned, for as Tuan (1993: 36) has observed, "Movement is thus like health, usually taken for granted until there is some lack in it."

This is how the sensory package involving re-learning how to run fast is depicted in one of our logs:

> Yesterday started speed work again and both noticed the difference immediately, not just in terms of the breathing becoming harder – more *burning*, but in terms of how our bodies' bits moved once more pace was injected: toes push ground *hard*, plantar fascia *moaning* at increased effort, extra *calf bulkin – relaxing*, ham strings getting bigger and smaller rapidly – feel their "*snap*," Achilles tendon *whipping* more. Arms *driving*. All is *whizzing, agitating, humming, drumming*. You can feel all of your body *buzzing* through the effort and extra blood flow... Interestingly today the areas that can be felt most by both of us are the adductors and hip flexors (inner thighs), they feel *sore* and *tight*, having been stretched in that way for the first time for ages. It feels good though, sort of the body remembering, or perhaps awakening itself to something it has done before. (Individual Log 1)

Leder (1990: 30–2) has perceptively depicted the phenomenological processes that make up the learning of corporeal skills, the combination of specific movement, sensation and cognition that he terms "incorporation." In our case, we were not developing a novel skill, but rediscovering an existing one that had been lost, temporarily at least. We had lost what Bourdieu (1990) might have termed our "feel for the game" of running performance. Via the rehabilitative program, we achieved the re-incorporation of our running skills made up of a sense of rhythm, timing and kinesthetic awareness. At this juncture we encounter another dimension of the distance runners' sensuous geography, that of their immediate "soundscape" (Rodaway 1994).

Listening to the Route

As previously noted, runners practice their running for practical purposes, and their concerns focus upon: (a) safety and (b) performance. Rodaway (1994: 95) has noted that "sound is not just sensation: it is information. We do not merely hear, we listen." Hence, hearing and listening are important for traversing ground efficiently. Runners become practiced at making auditory evaluations of the physical and social spaces they run through. Their primary concern is one of safety and, especially in urban areas, vehicles constitute a serious hazard. Crossing roads and junctions demands particular attention from the senses particularly on dark winter evenings:

> At the roundabout we concentrate monitoring traffic coming from three ways, the busiest direction cannot be seen as vehicles accelerate around a corner immediate to us, which is partially obscured by a large tree and hopeless street lighting. Their sound *Rrrrrrrrrrrrrrrrrrrah!* hits the brain, reverberating down the spine into the feet. When the sound is higher and more *aggressive*, we rock backwards and forwards, toe to heel, heel to toe, waiting for that gap in the traffic (Individual Log 2)

Parks in particular constitute public spaces in which dog-owners let their pets roam with impunity, much to the annoyance of distance runners who become highly attuned to the presence of dogs as they constitute a problematic feature of training runs. While experienced runners look out for dogs they also "listen" for them acutely:

> In my mind I can hear them coming, that Doberman Pinscher with teeth *bared* attack, a puppy causing me to spill over and most recently that Dalmatian *ramming* its shoulder into the back of my right hamstring sending me down on the local park. Always from behind initially, so the ears seem to have grown bigger over the years, attuned to them. I know what they sound like, they come quick, and their four feet are fast, different from humans, *pssshhhhhhhh,pssshhhhh* ... over the leaves. Their noise is riveted into my cortex, my synapses, hot-wired into my memory circuits. (Individual Log 1)

Monitoring sounds is important for running safety and also crucial for performance in terms of getting the maximum benefit from training sessions. Runners are concerned with how they are "going" in any particular training session. While the running body is propelled by a skeleton and musculature, it is also propelled by a respiratory system. Breath or respiration provides a constant and almost instantaneous feedback on the state of every training session, as runners listen to and evaluate their own breathing patterns. These patterns of inhalation and exhalation constitute the mechanism via which internal autonomic physiological processes interrelate with socially mediated or external processes (Lyon 1997). From the runner's point of view training sessions are categorized along a continuum ranging between negative and positive poles. Such categorization is partially enabled by an evaluation of breathing patterns, so respiration is intimately connected with the socially constituted normative order of accomplishing training. These patterns produce particular feeling or emotion states. There is, then, a direct relationship between respiratory patterns, the athlete's subjectivity (Lyon 1997: 96) and the judgments made to categorize sessions.

Distance running training is made up of a combination of aerobic and anaerobic work. The former consists of runs at a particular pace for a particular duration or time, and is designed to produce endurance. The latter is comprised of smaller but much more intense "efforts," which produce the capacity to run at speed. The combination of anaerobic and aerobic work produces effective racing performances. Runners then learn to associate particular kinds of breathing patterns with particular kind of sessions, and such patterns are correlated with individual pace thresholds. The nearer the pace threshold, the quicker and harder the breathing pattern, less effort produces less intense breathing. Once experienced, athletes possess considerable knowledge concerning what they should be able to achieve (in terms of time taken to cover distance) when doing particular sessions. They also develop a kinesthetic memory of how they should feel during those sessions, part of which includes the respiratory pattern. Sessions are always evaluated against these individual embodied standards. In addition, when regularly running particular training routes, individuals become very aware of the habitual patterns of breathing they manifest when encountering particular physical features (hills, ploughed fields etc). *How* they are breathing then becomes a major indicator of how they are "going" in a session. The prime means of evaluating breathing is located in the degree of fluency patterns of inhalation and exhalation exhibit at any particular juncture. Breathing might well be rapid, deep and painful during anaerobic work, but if the session is going well there will be a "flow" to the pattern of respiration. This flow is in effect a particular rhythm of respiration (Goodridge 1999: 43). Where there is no flow, when breathing is "ragged" or disjointed, whether during aerobic or anaerobic work, athletes are alerted to the fact that they are struggling to meet the session's objectives. Whether the going is bad or good produces different emotions ranging from exhilaration to anxiety, which in turn impacts upon the breathing patterns themselves (Tomkins 1962: 48). The following log entry depicts how physiological sensations intimately connect with the production of emotions, in this case those of embarrassment over a poor running performance:

> Nothing fancy, just get out there and run seven miles easy. The problems was it wasn't easy, felt out of sorts right from the start. Normally when going up the first hill I would just click into

it, shorten the stride, work the arms lean into it, get the rhythm going with the breathing. I couldn't do it though, I was all over the place like some overweight jogger! Uaaaaaaaaaaaaaaaaah! I could hear myself wheezing and moaning and gasping. It was a struggle all the way round and I *felt* embarrassed. (Individual Log 1)

Hearing and listening to their breathing patterns provides runners with a direct resource with which to evaluate the state of their physical being – embodied evidence upon which to base decisions as they move over their training routes: to increase or decrease the pace; to shorten the session or prolong it. Another auditory resource revealed by analyzing the data, are the sounds the running footfall makes on different kinds of surfaces. For example, the relative softness and smoothness of new tarmac facilitates a rhythmical cadence (Goodridge 1999) that produces a low sssssssssssshhhhh sound. This informs runners that their cadence is flowing, which in turn encourages pace injection. In contrast when the runner hits the concrete of pavement the sound is higher, more abrasive, with a slaaaaaaaaap or thwaaaaaaaaaaaaaack to the ear. The running over this kind of terrain is not so rhythmical or so easy on musculature. The sluuuuuuuuuck sound of slushy snow and the cruuuuuuuuuuuuunch of crisp, firm snow, help inform the runner how to navigate the optimal path for traversing the route safely and effectively. The first surface is difficult to achieve any rhythm on and not good for ankles, while on the second surface it is possible to move with ease and impunity. Thus, the memory store of the experienced distance runner contains a catalog of differing sound patterns co-related with the potential different kinds of surfaces have for performance and safety.

While runners need to be alert to their immediate soundscapes their olfactory receptors provide another embodied resource as they traverse their training terrain.

Smelling the Route

When runners train they produce and engage with immediate "smellscapes" (Classen et al. 1994: 97) particular to themselves and their routes. These consist of an amalgam of odors or aromas that change according to activity, space, place and atmospheric/seasonal conditions. Those odors relevant to distance runners help individuals substantiate their athletic identity in a number of ways: (a) in an embodied sense (b) in a biographical sense (c) in a space-time sense.

Distance running and racing is an embodied activity that requires systematic, routine, vigorous exercise. The result is that sweat pours from participants, and the body and its equipment become permeated with its odor. As Synnott (1993: 190) has noted, "odour is a natural sign of the self as both a physical and a moral being. The odour is a symbol of the self." Hence while smells are physical sensations they also carry with them moral evaluations. Thus in contemporary industrial society those who smell fragrant are good and those who smell bad are bad, or at least suspicious! There are exceptions to this general cultural evaluation, including how bodies are evaluated in sporting contexts (Synnott 1993: 273). The pungency that permeates distance running bodies and equipment is symbolic of training and racing effort, and recognized as so by runners:

> The weather has been bad for weeks and I have been wearing a gortex jacket and a thermal top underneath it – and the sweat pours out of me during every session. My crotch, back and armpits give off a kind of gross *ripe* smell and my kit is saturated with it. It's a stink I am used to, that is me when I am out there working hard, putting the miles in... (Individual Log 1)

This pungency acts to substantiate the salience of athletes distance-running identities (Stryker 1987), helping to define who they are to themselves (Classen et al. 1994: 113).

Tuan (1993: 57) has pointed out the capacity of smells to invoke memories: "Odour has this power to restore the past because, unlike the visual image, it is an encapsulated experience that has been left largely uninterpreted and underdeveloped." The aromas that permeate training smellscapes have the capacity to link runners with past elements in their athletic biographies. The smell of newly cut grass on parkland always invokes in me a period of several months training on South Wales parks in preparation for a marathon in which I won a prize thirty years ago. The whiff of dog excrement invokes in my training partner/co-researcher a more recent memory, of a rage-filled jettisoning of new training shoes in the aftermath of treading in the offending material during a dark winter evening, six-mile session. For me, the slightest hint of lilac tree aroma necessitates a training route detour and conjures up a memory of suffering a violent coughing fit resulting in aborting a training session. Other smells evoke mutual athletic memories as in the following example:

> Today we were running in the local park underneath the row of pines, to find some shade . It was the hottest day of the summer so far, and we could actually smell the pine scent, we both simultaneously grunted: "N.D." These are the initials of our favorite training location in western France; a perfect place, all flat, soft, smooth, pine needle covered tracks, in a forest backing onto a huge quiet beach. Out of nowhere the smell conjured up the same response, the same favourite memory of running there. (Individual Log 2)

These smells bring forth into the conscious mind past athletic memories that help to substantiate the distance-running identity in the running present.

John Hockey

The final feature of the running smellscape is concerned with the part odors play in marking the passage of the routes over which runners train. Psathas (1979: 224) has identified how maps are read as a "set of sequential particulars," physical markers such as hills, valleys etc. In a similar fashion, interrogation of the data indicated that our habitual training routes contained sets of smelt sequential particulars. What is smelt acts to locate us at particular points in the route(s), it marks where we are and how far we have to go. So, on one particular route the curry aroma emanating from an Asian restaurant tells us we are a mere 300 meters from finishing the session. The flood of vehicle pollution from a busy traffic interchange designates that we are barely at the start of a route, and that the relatively clean air of a park will soon be inhaled. The stink from algae rotting on a lake denotes the halfway point of a particular six mile run. Some routes contain more smelt markers than others, and differences are also

Less Noise. Better Hearing: An Outline of the Essentials of Architectural Acoustics for the Practicing Architect and Engineer. From the CCA exhibition *Sense of the City/Sensations Urbaines*, Collection Centre Canadien d'Architecture/ Canadian Centre for Architecture, Montréal

evident if runs are primarily street based – as with the aroma of starch blown from the extractor fan of a laundry. In addition, seasons impact upon these olfactory markers: the pungency of rotting tree mulch is a winter marker, while the sweetness of cut grass on particular park avenues is a summer one. The presence of these aromatic markers *en route* signals to us in a direct way where we are on the route, and we use them to "order the experience and understanding of space" (Classen et al. 1994: 98).

Seeing the Route

For most of us, the context that surrounds us as social actors is evaluated and interpreted using broad cultural codes (Rose 1993): we see in a particular way, using cultural resources. Furthermore, specific social groups employ distinctive "ways of seeing," for example, the ways in which women see public places (Brooks Gardner 1980), or how different occupational groups view their work situations (Bittner 1967). What is actually seen in these situations is dependent upon the knowledge that has been accumulated via previous experience of the activities themselves. Ways of seeing are structured by specific kinds of knowledge, which are in turn informed by the act of seeing itself, in a complex circular process. This active looking is necessary in order to accomplish the particular task(s) at hand. Through the embodied running of particular sequences of social space, training routes are constructed (Carr et al. 1992), and are dependent upon a specific, active way of seeing; each route forming part of a store of memory. In order to portray the kinds of visual practices distance runners use in order to accomplish training in an effective manner, the following section consists of a narrative depiction of one part of a favorite training route, and is based upon our field notes. The narrative itself portrays knowledge about that route, for runners often build up extensive and detailed knowledge of their training routes (Smith 1997). This knowledge also constructs *how* the route is seen in the process of running. Runners concerns when seeing are focused upon issues of safety and issues of performance. To carry out these activities runners are attentive to routes that allow them to maximize their training. They then accumulate knowledge of, and follow, particular routes while pursuing the latter objective. So, for example, a stretch of flat road may be prized for doing 100–400 meter efforts. It will also be prized if its surface is smooth, allowing fast cadence to flow. There is then a concern with the nature of the terrain one is training on, and what it will, or will not facilitate in terms of training performance. The term "going" is often used by runners to describe the terrain's capability, so for example "good going" or "lousy going" for particular stretches of terrain.

Another practical concern of runners in relation to training is safety. (Smith (1997) has perceptively identified the strategies runners use to deal with harassment, and on rare occasions assault, while training in public places.) Runners thus become attentive to particular locations (bars, pubs etc) on their routes where the risk of potential verbal/physical attack arises. This paper will depict some of these kinds of concern, and it will also depict a more encompassing and prevalent threat to safety that emanates from a combination of the physical features of the terrain and other human traffic, such as vehicle drivers and bicyclists and also (as forementioned) dogs, all of whom use the routes along with runners. From the runner's perspective, this combination routinely harbors features that can cause athletic injury, and resultant cessation of training and racing. These concerns of performance and safety are illustrated in the following narrative sections derived from both our individual logs:

> In a few yards I move off the grass on to a path, feeling its newly laid bitumen easy on my feet, heading for some ornamental gates. Cautiously, I slow down, knowing that with the narrowing of the path as it reaches the gates I am liable to encounter some combination of: parents with prams, mountain bikers with attitude, psychotic pets and deranged children, all with the capacity to shoot into my path and do me damage!
>
> ...Into the other park and up a little pitch, shortening the stride, working the quadriceps harder, hamstrings contracting sharply and grumbling, moving right all the time to avoid a marshy patch there for six months of the year, work the arms, murmuring "come on dig in a bit." A bigger slope is before me, up the grass past the tennis courts, smooth all over now, any line taken will do. Good for doing hill repeats here... Along the park-top, going good, summer hazard arises due to mini golf – be aware! Reach a big clump of trees around which in winter is a boggy morass, producing freezing, sodden shoes, and sore Achilles' tendons as one's heels get sucked down too far in the mud. In summer there are great hardened ruts which do nothing for shin muscles which can get inflamed all too easily.

As Emmison and Smith (2000: 185) note, "environments are not simply places where we see things in a passive way. They are also locations where we must look in active ways." Runners see in active ways so as to make sense of the places of their training. Moreover, as Ingold (2000: 226, 230) has asserted "people see as they move" and "our knowledge of the environment undergoes continuous formation in the very course of [our] moving about in it." Hopefully, the preceding narrative passage has conveyed something of the runner's vision in movement. The paper now turns to examining how athletes touch their training terrain.

Feeling the Route
Runners traverse their training grounds, they touch that ground and in turn are touched by it, so there is a reciprocal haptic relationship between the runner and the world in terms of the route. Rodaway

(1994: 48) defines the haptic experience as "a combination of tactile and locomotive properties [that] provides information about the character of objects, surfaces and whole environments as well as our own bodies." The runner's touch is mainly an active one, combining pressure between the athletic body and the ground and a kinesthetic awareness of the body as it moves. "Touch is therefore, about both an awareness of presence and of locomotion" (Rodaway, 1994: 42). In addition, humans touch, as Hetherington (2003: 7) notes, "to confirm it: that it is there, that it feels like this... Touch is a way of removing doubt – of confirming." It is a directly embodied way of *feeling* the world and understanding its properties. Interestingly, as Ingold (2004: 330-331) points out, "studies of haptic perception have focused almost exclusively on manual touch" and he calls for the development of studies that examine the relationships between the environment and "techniques of footwork." The following is a narrative sequence derived from both individual logs that depicts the response of our feet to feeling differing kinds of terrain:

> *Zinnnnnnnnnnnnnnnnnnnnnng* goes my plantar fascia as I ouch! Hitting the ridges of malformed pavement, onto a less odious section, but the feet still resonate with slaaaaaaaaaaping and *burn* from the concrete – it gives you nothing.
>
> Down through the field feeling my way, summer grass is long and I move my toes searching out the contours of the hidden bumps of dry earth, careful and slow as some are big and the ankles roll, roll, rolling off them – ligaments strainiiing to compenseate, feel them m-o-a-n-I-n-g...
>
> I am running on air, six miles of *plush*, my feet bits are relaaaaaaaxed, no tension, every ligament, tendon and muscle *flowing* – smoooooooooooothly down the level pine needle caressed forest path. The ground giving me back *bounce* it's so cushioned.

The feet, while admittedly clad in running shoes, still feel the ground, perceiving its shape, size, texture and temperature, in effect its response to being trodden on. The slap of concrete resonates through the sole, the shape of items strode over are felt as the toes and forefoot grasp them, the feet swell and get hot as the temperature rises, and the tendons at the bottom of the ankle stretch more as boggy terrain is traversed. It is the running feet that feel, and that make constant, small, improvised adjustments to footfall, "tuning" (Ingold 2004: 332) in to the constantly changing properties (chosen path, climatic conditions etc) of training routes. Evaluating the route is, then, not just a visual process but also a haptic one, because feeling the ground provides athletes with information with which to categorize routes, and sections of routes, in terms of how conducive they are to safety, performance – and of course pleasure (Bale 2004: 74).

The running feet are not the only tactile part to *feel* the route, for the skin does also, exposed as it is to the varying weather conditions that form part of the particular training routes. As Montagu (1971) has shown, the skin provides the largest area of touch in the human body. Thus, runners are touched perennially by heat, wet, cold and air as the elements bombard them. This passive process of being touched tends to be greater in the late spring and the summer as runners exchange hats, gloves and track suits for shorts and vests. However, even in the depths of winter, swaddled in layers, runners feel the elements, which often make the traversing of routes more arduous:

> Tonight into the poorly lit streets like gladiators all swathed in waterproof gear against wet snow. Our hands still *freeze* despite two pairs of gloves, they a-c-h-e sooooo much, it's like having foreign objects at the end of oneself! The only exposed bits are our faces. It's not so bad down the streets but alongside the exposed side of the park the wind drives the snow directly at us and it *feels* like gravel being rubbbbbbbbed into you, like your skin is burrrrrrrrrning, and when we get indoors our cheeks are bright red like circus clowns! (Individual Log 2)

Runners touch and are touched by the ground they traverse and this two way process builds an embodied relationship with their training terrain. Where they perceive themselves as belonging to and being part of their habitual routes, part of those particular combinations of space, place, time and distance (Rodaway 1994: 54).

Conclusion

This paper has portrayed how the senses are experienced and used by distance runners in the particular social space (Lefebvre 1991) of their habitual training routes. Using data from a two-year collaborative autoethnographic project the paper has portrayed how the central concerns of safety and performance are assessed and acted upon by runners, using cognitive and corporeal information accrued by their senses. These sensory patterns do not work in isolation (Merleau-Ponty 1962) but are interlocking and mutually influential. The substance of the body, its very flesh, interacts with the fabric of the social world. Runners' physical engagement with the world is via a subcultural stock of learnt practical techniques and meanings. These are enacted in the particular sections of space and time that are corporeally known and cognitively categorized as "training routes." How distance runners see a hill as it approaches them, what the ground feels like as they ascend it, how their cadence changes as they engage with it, what the odor of their own sweat means to them as they labor up it and what their lungs tell them at the top of it – these cognitive and corporeal ways of knowing unfold as the route does itself.

It is hoped that this account gives some indication of the particular sensory complexity of "sensing the run." Given there is little phenomenological or ethnomethodological literature on physical activity or sport, there would be seem to be fertile grounds for charting and analyzing the sensory dimensions of these areas of social life.

Acknowledgment
The author wishes to thank the reviewers and his co-runner and co-researcher Dr Jacquelyn Allen Collinson, for their helpful comments and suggestions on an earlier draft.

Note
1. There have of course been autobiographical (Bannister 2004) and fictional (Sillitoe 1993) depictions of distance running that, while not analytic, have been evocative of embodied experience.

References
Allen Collinson, J. 2005. "Emotions, Interaction and the Injured Sporting Body." *International Review for the Sociology of Sport*, 40: 221–40.

—— and Hockey, J. 2001. "Runners' Tales: Autoethnography, Injury and Narrative." *Auto/Biography*, IX: 95–106.

—— and —— 2005. "Autoethnography: Self-indulgence or Rigorous Methodology?" In M. MacNamee (ed.) *Philosophy and the Sciences of Exercise, Health and Sport*. London: Routledge.

Bale, J. 2004. *Running Cultures: Racing in Time and Space*. London: Routledge.

Bannister, R. 2004. *The First Four Minutes*. Stroud: Sutton.

Benson, D. and Hughes, J. A. 1983. *The Perspective of Ethnomethodology*. London: Longman.

Bittner, E. 1967. "The Police on Skid Row." *Sociological Review*, 2: 699–715.

Bourdieu, P. 1990. *The Logic of Practice*. Cambridge: Polity.

Brooks Gardner, C. 1980. "Passing By: Street Remarks, Address Rights, and the Urban Female." *Sociological Inquiry*, 50: 328–56.

Carr, S., Francis, M., Rivlin, L. and Stone, A. 1992. *Public Space*. Cambridge: Cambridge University Press.

Classen, C. 1997. "Foundations for an Anthropology of the Senses." *International Social Science Journal*, 49: 401–12.

——, Howes, D. and Synott, A. 1994. *Aroma: The Cultural History of Smell*. London: Routledge.

Coates, S. 1999. "Analysing the Physical: An Ethnomethodological Study of Boxing." *Ethnographic Studies*, 4: 14–26

Coffey, A. 1999. *The Ethnographic Self*, London: Sage.

Crossley, N. 1995. "Merleau-Ponty, the Elusive Body and Carnal Sociology." *Body & Society*, 1: 43–63.

—— 2001. *The Social Body: Habit, Identity and Desire*, London: Sage.

Denison, J. and Rinehart, R. 2000. "Introduction: Imagining Sociological Narratives." *Sociology of Sport Journal,* 17: 1–4.

Downey, G. 2005. *Learning Capoeira. Lessons from an Afro-Brazilian Art*. Oxford: Oxford University Press.

Emmison, M. and Smith, P. 2000. *Researching the Visual. Images, Objects, Contexts and Interactions in Social and Cultural Enquiry*. London: Sage.

Feher, M. 1987. "Of Bodies and Technologies." In H. Foster (ed.) *Discussions in Contemporary Culture No.1*. Dia Art Foundation, Seattle: Seattle Bay Press.

Gibson, J. 1966. *The Senses Considered as a Perceptual System*. Boston, MA: Houghton Mifflin.

Glaser, B. and Strauss, A. 1967. *The Discovery of Grounded Ttheory*. Chicago: Aldine.

Goodridge, J. 1999. *Rhythm and Timing of Movement in Performance*. London: Jessica Kingsley.

Hetherington, K. 2003. *Spatial Textures: Places, Touch and Praesentia*, Lancaster: Department of Sociology, Lancaster University. Available online: http://www.comp.lancs.ac.uk/sociology/papers/Hetherington-Spatial-Textures.pdf

Hockey, J. 2005. "Injured Distance Runners: A Case of Identity Work as Self-Help." *Sociology of Sport Journal* , 21 : 38–58.

Howes, D. 2003. *Sensual Relations. Engaging the Senses in Cultural and Social Theory*. Ann Arbor: University of Michigan Press.

—— 2005. "Introduction." In D. Howes (ed.) *Empire of the Senses: The Sensual Culture Reader*. Oxford: Berg.

Ingold, T. 2000. *The Perception of the Environment. Essays in Livelihood, Dwelling and Skill*, London: Routledge.

—— 2004. "Culture on the Ground: The World Perceived Through the Feet." *Journal of Material Culture*, 9: 315–40.

Kerry, D. S. and Armour, K. M. 2000. "Sport Sciences and the Promise of Phenomenology: Philosophy, Method, and Insight." *Quest, 52*: 1–17.

Kew, F. 1986. "Playing the Game: An Ethnomethodological Perspective." *International Review for the Sociology of Sport* 21: 305–21.

Leder, D. 1990. *The Absent Body*. Chicago: University of Chicago Press.

Lefebvre, H. 1991. *The Production of Social Space*. 2nd edn. Translated by D. Nicholson-Smith. Malden, MA: Blackwell.

Lewis, N. 2000. "The Climbing Body, Nature and the Experience of Modernity." *Body & Society*, 6: 58–80.

Lyon, M.L. 1997. "The Material Body, Social Processes and Emotion: 'Techniques of the Body' Revisited." *Body & Society*, 3: 83–101.

Merleau-Ponty, M. 1962. *Phenomenology of Perception*. Translated by C. Smith. London: Routledge & Kegan Paul.

Montagu, A. 1971. *Touching: The Human Significance of Skin*. New York: Columbia University Press.

Psathas, G. 1979. "Organizational Features of Direction Maps." In G. Psathas (ed.) *Everyday Language: Studies in Ethnomethodology*. New York: Irvington.

Rodaway, P. 1994. *Sensuous Geographies: Body, Sense and Place*. London: Routledge.

Rose, G. 1993. *Feminism and Geography: The Limits of Geographical Knowledge*. Cambridge: Polity Press.

Rotella, C. 2002. *Good With Their Hands: Boxers, Bluesmen, and Other Characters from the Rust Belt*. Berkeley: University of California Press.

Ryave, A. L. and Schenkein, J. N. 1975. "Notes on the Art of Walking." In R. Turner (ed.) *Ethnomethodology: Selected Readings*. Harmondsworth: Penguin.

Sillitoe, A. 1993. *The Loneliness of the Long Distance Runner*. London: Flamingo.

Smith, G. 1997. "Incivil Attention and Everyday Tolerance: Vicissitudes of Exercising in Public Places." *Perspectives on Social Problems*, 9: 59–79.

Smith, S.L. 1998. "Athletes, Runners, and Joggers: Participant–group Dynamics in a Sport of Individuals." *Sociology of Sport Journal*, 15: 174–92.

Stewart, L. 1995. "Bodies, Visions and Spatial Politics: A Review Essay on Henri Lefebvre's The Production of Space." *Environment and Planning D: Society and Space*, 13: 609–18.

Stryker, S. 1987. "Identity Theory: Developments and Extensions." In K. Yardley and T. Honess (eds) *Identity: Self and Psychosocial Perspectives*. New York: John Wiley.

Synnott, A. 1993. *The Body Social: Symbolism, Self and Society*. London: Routledge.

Sudnow, D. N. 1972. "Temporal Parameters of Interpersonal Observation." In D. Sudnow (ed.) *Studies in Social Interaction*. New York: Free Press.

Tomkins, S.S. 1962. *Affect, Imagery, Consciousness, Vol. I (The Positive Affects)*. New York: Springer.

Tuan, Y.F. 1993. *Passing Strange and Wonderful*. Washington, DC: Island Press-Shearwater.

Wacquant, L. 2004. *Body And Soul: Notebooks of an Apprentice Boxer*. Oxford: Oxford University Press.

Celebrate the 10th anniversary of Fashion Theory

The Journal of Dress, Body & Culture

Edited by Dr. Valerie Steele, Director of the Museum at the Fashion Institute of Technology in New York

'A fine addition to academic institutions with cultural studies programs; essential for those with special collections in fashion and costume.' **Library Journal**

'Fashion Theory is both chic and serious – yes, and sexy, too.' **Times Higher Education Supplement**

'For those who dismiss fashion as frivolous, here's proof otherwise.' **Harper's Bazaar**

Reprinted courtesy of Arkadius

Since its launch in 1997 as the first journal devoted to the intellectual understanding of the dressed body, *Fashion Theory* has remained at the vanguard of international fashion scholarship.

Celebrate Fashion Theory's 10th anniversary with

- NEW online only pricing - $200 / £115
- Volumes 1-6 will be available online from March 2007, completing the online archive
- A NEW annotated index of all articles in Volume 10 Issue 4!
- A NEW *Fashion Theory* Reader in 2007 – selected highlights from 10 years!
- A NEW *Fashion Theory* Set – 27 issues for 15% off! ONLY $665 / £375!

FASHION THEORY ISSN 1362-704X	1 year
Individual Subscription Print only, does not include online access.	£46 / $79
Institutional Print and Online Includes online access Vol. 7-10.	£140 / $250
Online only Includes online access Vol. 7-10.	£115+VAT / $200
The Print Set Volumes 1-7	£375 / $665

Indexed by:
IBSS, DAAI, ART Bibliographies Modern, H.W. Wilson Art Index, AIO, Sociological Abstracts, ISI Web of Science/Arts & Humanities Citation Index, THOMSON ISI Current Contents Connect/Arts & Humanities, MLA Bibliography.

Published 4 times a year in March, June, September and December.

BERG

Order online at www.bergpublishers.com or call +44(0)1767 604951
Institutional subscriptions include online access through www.IngentaConnect.com
To order a sample copy please contact enquiry@bergpublishers.com
View issue 7.1 free online at www.ingentaconnect.com

See It, Sense It, Save It: Economies of Multisensuality in Contemporary Zoos

Nils Lindahl Elliot

Dr Nils Lindahl Elliot is a senior lecturer in the School of Cultural Studies at UWE, Bristol. From 2002 to 2005 he was principal investigator in an ESRC-funded project entitled "The New Zoos: Science, Media & Culture." His first book-length analysis on the subject of the mass mediation of nature will appear in *Mediating Nature* (Routledge 2006).
Nils.Lindahl-Elliot@uwe.ac.uk

ABSTRACT Contemporary zoos publicize their role as centers for the conservation of endangered species and include so-called "naturalistic displays." These and other aspects of the new zoos can be fruitfully analyzed from the perspective of what some analysts describe as the predominance of "visual culture" in modern societies. The following essay nonetheless makes the case for an interpretation of zoos that highlights their multisensual character. On the basis of the semeiotic theory of Charles Sanders Peirce and the results of visitor research at two British zoos, the essay develops an account that articulates four different modalities of observation and their corresponding economies of multisensuality.

The Marie Le Fevre Ape Centre at the Paignton Zoo Environmental Park is a good example of a newer generation of zoo displays[1] that combine what the industry describes as environmental enrichment with naturalistic landscaping. Environmental enrichment refers to the provision of the environmental stimuli that zoologists deem to be required for a specimen's "optimal psychological and physiological well-being" (Shepherdson 1998: 1). In turn, naturalistic landscaping refers to a form of display design that simulates the habitat of the species. While there is no automatic continuity between these two practices, the promotional discourses of zoos frequently work to establish an association between them: naturalistic landscaping equates with environmental enrichment, or at least, with animal welfare.

The Paignton Zoo's display, designed to house the zoo's western lowland gorillas and Bornean orangutans, includes a large outdoor area with numerous trees, a pond, ropes between trees for climbing, as well as a gorilla's equivalent of a jungle gym and an indoor shelter for the nonhuman animals. Visitors can use a variety of purpose-built viewing areas to see the animals from afar, but the indoor shelter also affords them with close-up views of both species. In 1998 Jane Goodall presented the zoo with a Zoo Animal Welfare Award for the exhibit, and some seven years later, it is still one of the zoo's most popular attractions.

The display's indoor viewing area is also a marvelously smelly place. In the course of conducting ethnographic research with some thirty-five families at this and at the Bristol Zoo,[2] it became apparent to me that especially the younger visitors had a strong reaction to this aspect of the display. In most cases the reactions involved exclamations such as "Phew! It's *smelly* Mummy!" or, as one older child put it, "They should use some *air freshener* in here!" In a few cases there was a stronger response: four of the children refused to go into this, and indeed into *any* of the more pungently aromatic displays in either zoo, and the parents of one family reported that one of their children had begun to retch the first time that they entered the Ape Centre.

Now it might be inferred from this account that the odors in the display made for a negative visiting experience. The epithet "smelly zoo" has long been used to denigrate zoos. But while some of the children responded with physical revulsion to the smells, many, if not most reacted with a mixture of surprise, disgust *and delight:* here was something not only out of the ordinary, but something that provoked a paradoxical pleasure, not least from the perspective of the transgressive possibilities of "dirt" (Douglas 1991).

Many zoos around the world now attempt to incorporate the sense of smell as part of what might be described as an ecological "pedagogy of the senses." For example, the Chester Zoo's "Spirit of the Jaguar" display includes "scent boxes" for visitors which contain, among other scents, vanilla and what is reportedly a synthetic version of jaguar urine.[3] The Paignton Zoo has itself organized a trail called the "Senses Hunt" that is designed to teach children how animals use their senses to survive. And the Bristol Zoo Gardens include a number of displays – the zoo's so-called "zoolympics" – that invite visitors to instrumentalize a variety of their senses. While my research focused on two British zoos, similar practices are commonly found in many zoos throughout the world.

If it is true that all social practices tend to involve a degree of multisensuality, it seems that zoos are multisensual visitor attractions *par excellence.* And yet, any newcomer to the growing cultural and historical literature about zoos – especially zoos that have embraced what I described earlier as naturalistic landscaping – might be forgiven for assuming that zoos are designed and visited for their *visual* pleasures, and, thereby, for their enactment of what a number of scholars now describe as "visual culture."

In the following essay I should like to provide a somewhat different account of the nature of zoos, one that offers a network of concepts with which to describe what might be described as contemporary zoos' *economy of multisensuality*. Here I refer not so much to the modern notion of "economy" – though certainly many zoos attempt to commodify their most explicit multisensualities – but to two older meanings of the word: economy as a certain arrangement of something, and, in the archaic sense of the word, as the management of household affairs. Derived from *ménage*, meaning "household" in the original French, and also household management in English, the older name for zoos is, of course, "menagerie." The notion of an economy of multisensuality might thereby be described as the sensual equivalent of a zoo's management of a collection of animals: the different senses themselves appear to be "collected" and "managed," if not "domesticated."

The Zoo of "Visual Culture"

I have emphasized the multisensuality of zoos. I would, however, like to begin my analysis by acknowledging the case for an analysis that privileges the visual dimension of representation and observation in zoos. I refer to this as a "visual culture" analysis. While there is no single widely accepted definition or delimitation for just what constitutes "visual culture," I take it that the term refers to the ostensive prevalence of the visual sense in modern cultures.[4] We can agree provisionally with Marita Sturken and Lisa Cartwright when they suggest that "[t]he world we inhabit is filled with visual images" and that such images are "central to how we represent, make meaning, and communicate in the world around us"; or indeed when they suggest that "in many ways … our culture is an increasingly visual one" (Sturken and Cartwright 2001: 1).

I take it that the "we" and the "our" in these statements refer especially, but not only to the world inhabited by the authors, and by many if not most readers of their book and indeed of this essay. I

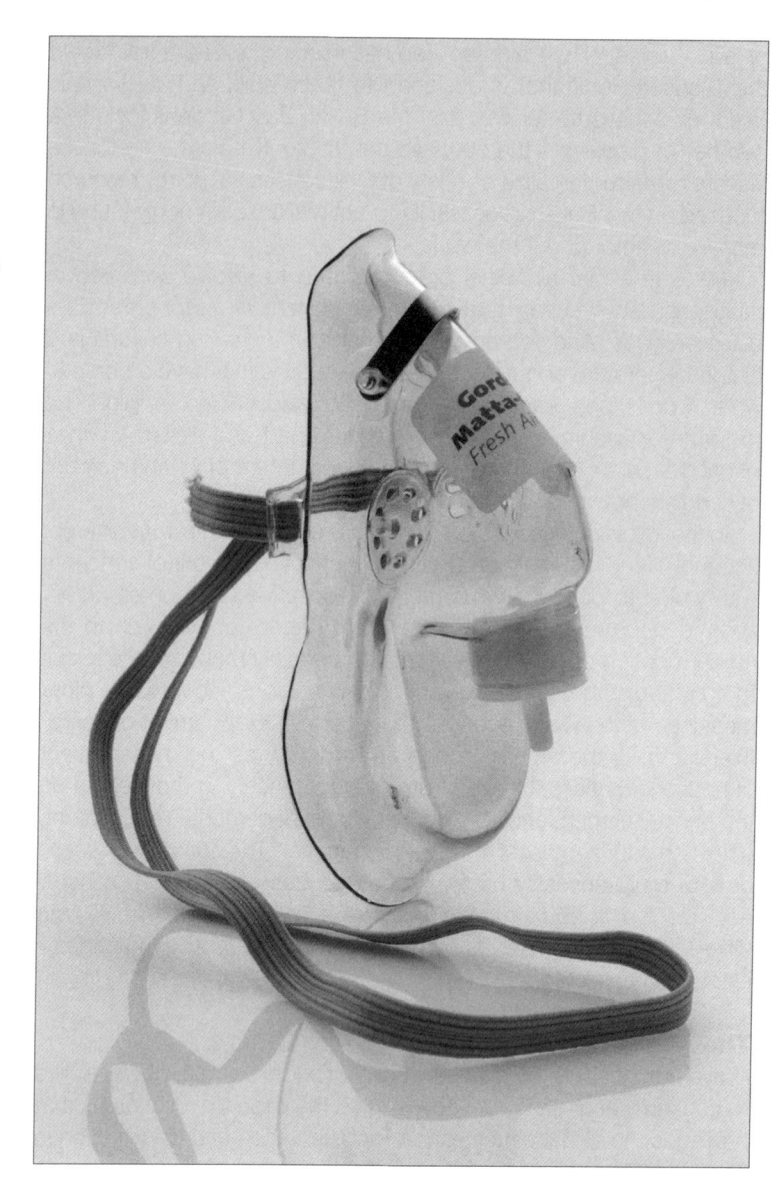

Fresh Air Cart Mask. From the CCA exhibition *Sense of the City/Sensations Urbaines*, © Centre Canadien d'Architecture/ Canadian Centre for Architecture, Montréal Photo Michel Boulet

also take it that most if not all studies of visual culture are premised, at least in the context of cultural and media studies, on what might be described as a "social constructivist" epistemology: the description and analysis of visual culture assumes a shift from what Irit Rogoff describes as the "old logical-positivist world of cognition" to "a more contemporary arena of representation and situated knowledges" (Rogoff 2002: 26–7). If it is true that "our" world is intensively and extensively mediated with and by visual images, then one of the tasks for cultural theorists is to elucidate the manner in which such images are produced, constructed, circulated and appropriated in particular social contexts.

At first glance, zoos would appear to be a particularly strong example of "visual culture." Even before visitors reach a zoo, they are likely to begin to get a visual sense of the zoo by way of photographic images. Zoo leaflets have, almost as a rule, a full-color photograph of one or more charismatic animals on their front side. A variety of other visual media are also employed to entice audiences to visit zoos: for example, the Bristol Zoo advertises itself by placing gigantic images of its different animals on Bristol's double-decker buses and in 2003 the London Zoo dressed up several London Taxis in leopard spots and snake scales to promote its own site. Such promotional strategies are used by many zoos across the world and may well be interpreted as signs of the prevalence of visual culture. They are also the unmistakable signs of the adoption by zoos of more and more sophisticated forms of marketing, merchandizing and consumer segmentation in what is an increasingly crowded and competitive leisure industry.

Now the mission statements of many contemporary zoos are premised on what I describe as a discourse of environmental realism. An analysis of this discourse is beyond the scope of this essay.[5] Instead, I would like to highlight the fact that this discourse is corresponded by the extensive reproduction, in both promotional images and in the displays themselves, of the photographic *naturalism*[6] associated with the *National Geographic* and other "nature media" – a comparatively small group of media corporations such as the BBC and Disney that have played a preeminent role not only in the representation of nature, but indeed in the definition of what counts *as* "nature" (Lindahl Elliot 2006). It is, in this sense, no accident that two significant sites for the promotion of the most recent design principles have involved the work of Michael "Nick" Nichols, a *National Geographic* photographer who specializes in the representation of "wild" natures such as the Ndoki region of Central Africa.[7]

Key features of this form of naturalism include a privileging of "wild" natures, i.e. natures that can be represented as being "untouched," "pristine," "Edenic" or "Arcadian"; a tacit conception of observation as being primarily (if not exclusively) a matter of *visual* practice; and, as part of this, a form of visualization that generally does not encourage self-reflexivity with respect to the observational process itself.[8]

This form of naturalism is evident in the promotional strategies that I mentioned above – in and for which animals tend to be photographed either in the wild, or in ways that dissimulate their enclosure. But it also shapes the predominant design discourse and indeed the actual geography of many contemporary displays, which, as I noted earlier, are premised on principles of "naturalistic" landscaping. It is, in this sense, possible to establish a strong relation of *transmediation* between this style, and the photographic naturalism I have just alluded to. I define transmediation as the transposition of modalities of observation, or aspects of modalities of observation associated with one context, to another (Lindahl Elliot 2006). The transmediation of the photographic naturalism in question means that the displays tend to emulate one of a finite set of habitats associated with "wild" nature. In this context, rainforests and other habitats privileged by the nature media occupy pride of place; moreover, the displays are designed to dissimulate the boundaries between the visitor and the visited, but also between the display and the wider environ of the zoo. This is achieved by means of a variety of devices, which include discrete forms of electric fencing, netting with a very fine filament, as well as the extensive use of foliage and other "natural" barriers such as ponds. While such displays are occasionally accompanied by accounts of the manner in which certain enclosure design techniques benefit the specimens on display, more often than not their actual signs encourage the visitor to become more reflexive with respect to the habitat and the species, and *not* with respect to the form of enclosure, let alone the own role in the observation, or indeed the symbolic commodification of the wildlife on display.

Last but not least, the displays are arguably an instance of transmediation insofar as they are designed to provide above all else, a *visual,* if not only visual, sense of "wilderness." As one zoo landscape designer explained in a recent zoo design symposium, "[i]n order for something to be perceived as realistic or natural, we must provide the necessary *visual* cues to support the message, without exception" (McClintock 2005:37, my emphasis). Attention to the design of a zoo display

> requires the same attention as a landscape painting. The artist will compose the scene to include a foreground (greatest detail and sharpest colours), a middle ground (often the main focus) and a background (least detail and muted colours). Without any one of these elements, the scene will appear flat, without depth (McClintock 2005: 38).

Zoo critics have long suggested that the primary motivation for the emphasis on naturalistic displays can be found in the zoo industry's need to address the challenge of animal rights activism. As I began to suggest earlier, the development of such a "painterly" form of naturalism – the metaphor and techniques are of course themselves forms of transmediation – is commonly equated, at least in promotional discourses, with environmental enrichment. However, and as a group of researchers at the Paignton Zoo noted, "many modern and expensive zoo enclosures may not meet the needs of the animals as they do those of visitors and staff"; one of the reasons for this is that "in recent years the visitor experience has become the overwhelming consideration in zoo design" Melfi et al. 2005).

The official history of the design and development of Disney's Animal Kingdom, a trend-setting nature theme park that Disney opened in 1998, is illuminating in this respect. As Melody Malmberg, the author of the official history of the making of the park put it, Disney brought in an "animal expert" only after its design team began work on the safari ride, and when its "imagineers" began to ask questions about "[h]ow animals could be encouraged to be active, to cluster in a *picturesque* and *viewable* valley, to interact?" (Malmberg 1998: 24, my emphasis). Concerned that animal welfare was being overlooked, the animal expert felt compelled to call in colleagues from other zoos for what Malmberg describes as a "series of long, spirited meetings" (Malmberg 1998:26).

At least in the case of Disney's Animal Kingdom, zoo designers were certainly under instructions to differentiate the new park from zoos. As Malmberg explains, Disney imaginers visited a number of zoos and animal facilities, "paying attention to naturalistic exhibits and areas of contact between guests and animals, noting what worked and what didn't"; "each time they returned to Imagineering, they had to explain how and why Disney's Animal Kingdom Theme Park would *not* be a zoo" (Malmberg 1998: 16). Presumably Disney did not wish its new theme park to be associated with the stigma of the older zoos.

However, in Disney's Animal Kingdom and in many other zoos, this is arguably just one of a rather more complex set of motivations that have informed zoo design since at least the late 1960s when the latest forms of naturalism began to emerge in the United States. The imagineers at the Disney Corporation would doubtless have been as keen to dissimulate the "zoo-ness" of their zoo as they were to produce a *spectacular* nature in the sense of spectacle defined by Guy Debord (1995), i.e. a nature premised on the logic of an "immense accumulation of spectacles" for which and in which "all that once was directly lived has [now] become representation" (Debord 1995: 12).

From this perspective, contemporary zoos are now sites for the production of *images* of nature. In Debord's terms, such images are increasingly "detached from every aspect of life," "apprehended in a *partial* way" and conducive to a "concrete inversion of life" insofar as "reality unfolds in a new generality as a pseudo-world apart, solely as an object of contemplation" (Debord 1995: 12). Zoo critics might thereby argue that contemporary zoo displays should be regarded not so much as sites for a pedagogy of conservationism but, in the terms of Susan Davis (1997), as "spectacles of nature," that is to say, as one of the many sites in modern culture devoted to the commodification of nature. It goes almost without saying that the campaigns of many environmentalist organizations – most notably, Greenpeace – might equally be interpreted in this manner.

The Semeiotic Zoo

In this essay I will not consider the merits of such a critique with respect to zoos' pedagogic discourses; instead, I will explore a number of epistemological and methodological issues raised by such an analysis. While my brief analysis sheds some light on what we might describe with Henri Lefebvre (1991) as the "conceived" space of zoos – what he calls the representation of space – it says little or nothing about what Lefebvre describes as "perceived" and "lived" space. Equally if not more importantly, it says little or nothing about "natural" space. And of course, it says nothing about what I have described as the multisensuality of zoos.

All of these omissions are problematic, but perhaps the most problematic one involves the nature of natural space, or what might be described more generally as material nature. Zoo displays do not just involve "images" of nature. Unlike television documentaries and wildlife photography, zoos involve a more-than-symbolic, more-than-representational nature. Any analysis of zoo displays must thus begin by explaining *how* zoos are more-than-representational and what consequences this has for an analysis of the displays, and indeed for visitors' observational practices.

Doing so poses a number of challenges, especially in a research context that, as I noted earlier, is premised on a constructivist epistemology. Many researchers assume that realism and naturalism are inherently problematic, and much of their work is devoted to critiques of the methodology and indeed ideology associated with them. Perhaps for this reason, questions about the "real" physicality of non-human animals, about their status as natural or quasi-natural entities, their differences from human animals and their effects on visitors are either taken for granted, or attacked as being inherently – we might say, paradoxically, "essentially" – problematic. But as W.J.T. Mitchell has noted in his critique of "visual culture," it is just as important to critique the naturalistic fallacy as it is to critique dogmatic critiques of the naturalistic fallacy. "A dialectical concept of visual culture," Mitchell suggests, "expects that the very notion of vision as a *cultural* activity necessarily entails an investigation of its non-cultural dimensions" (Mitchell 2002: 92). Speaking more generally of the culturalism[9] that arguably now dominates cultural theory, Kate Soper (1995) makes an analogous point when she critiques the tendency in much cultural theory to reduce nature to culture. Soper suggests that, however much it is necessary to question the divide between nature and culture, nature and humanity, the conceptual distinction remains indispensable. She further argues that it is necessary to recognize the existence of a material nature whose structures and processes continue to be independent of human activity. This in the sense that they are not a humanly created product, and that they remain the condition for human existence (Soper 1995: 132–3).

Mitchell's and Soper's critiques seem particularly relevant in the context of zoos. Accounts of zoo animals that treat them as no more than representations – or indeed as culture–nature hybrids for which culture has the last hand – overlook the fact that zoo animals die, and thereby that the morphologies and even the ethologies of zoo animals are still determined by a material nature that is not so easily incorporated as part of discursive, technological or institutional networks. The point is not to deny that zoo animals are *represented* in zoos, or indeed that by being placed in zoos they begin to be incorporated as part of such networks. Indeed it is clear that as part of this process, the behavior, and even some aspects of the morphologies of zoo animals do undergo some change. Rather, the point is to critique forms of research that go so far as to suggest that animals in zoos lose all or most of their material nature, in the sense defined by Soper. While few scholars would go to the extent of adopting the last stance explicitly, their silence on the matter frequently means that animals in zoos are all too easily reduced, however implicitly, to the status of representational entities.

Now, if the nature of zoo animals is more-than-representational and does involve something like a "material nature," then it must be true that the nature of zoo displays, and indeed of *observational* processes in zoos, must themselves be more-than-symbolic, and must involve, in some shape or form, a material nature. A similar point might well be made with respect to the nature of multisensuality, and indeed the nature of the observational process itself. Stating this otherwise obvious point is relatively simple – articulating it as part of a critical analysis of multisensuality in zoos is another matter.

In my own research I have found it useful to address aspects of this problem with reference to the phenomenology and semeiotic theory[10] of Charles Sanders Peirce (1931–58; 1992; 1998), two aspects of whose work seem particularly useful in the context of an analysis of zoos. The first of these is Peirce's phenomenology, as articulated by his categories of firstness, secondness and thirdness. Returning to the example with which I began this essay, we might suggest that observing a gorilla entails at once a process of naming by way of signs (what Peirce described as the dimension of "thirdness"); a dynamic of action and reaction such as occurs when visitors are struck by a strong sense of smell or respond by way of reflex actions to a sudden movement by the animal (what Peirce described as "secondness"); but also the relative i-mediacy of feeling: for example, seeing an animal for the first time and being left speechless by its strangeness (what Peirce described as "firstness").

Far from being mutually exclusive, all three of these aspects are mutually imbricating: the nature of thirdness presupposes (but is not reducible to) the nature of secondness, which in turn presupposes (but is itself not reducible to) the nature of firstness. Put differently, from a phenomenological perspective firstness is always becoming secondness and secondness is always becoming thirdness. It seems to me that this phenomenological framework goes a long way towards addressing the critique of culturalism; while secondness does not necessarily involve relations of or with material nature, it does involve both "less-than-semeiotic" and "more-than-semeiotic" qualities that are frequently overlooked by representational analyses. At the same time, the category of firstness recognizes the significance of affect and emotion even as it preserves the possibility of a degree of indetermination in both social and natural processes.

The second aspect of Peirce's theory is related to the first, and involves his semeiotic theory. While textbook primers in semiotics sometimes attempt to establish a series of equivalences with de Saussure's sign model, Peirce's theory escapes the logocentrism of Saussure, and crucially, its neglect of the question of referentiality. Peirce's triadic sign model is premised on the notion that signs involve a three-way relation between a sign-object (which may include an empirical object), a representamen (which may be a nonhuman animal) and an interpretant: the necessary translation of signs into other signs. Peirce's most famous typology of signs – signs as symbols, indexes and icons – allows in turn for the possibility of signs that are, as he describes it, in a real relation with their objects, but also, objects that are in a real relation with their interpretants.

When, for example, a child experiences the smell, holds her or his nose, and says "Phew! It's smelly in here," she or he produces a sign that is at once a conventional symbol insofar as it entails the use of words; an index that "points out" the smell and aspects of which are in a real physical relation to the smell; and an icon, that is to say a likeness of the sense of surprise and revulsion felt at the smell: the child's parents can see the child holding her/his nose (which is itself of course a conventional sign), but can also *hear* the surprise in the exclamation even as they themselves sense the pungent smell.[11] By this account, icons – and indeed all of Peirce's semeiotic categories – are by no means exclusively a matter of visuality: a pungent smell, a loud noise or indeed touching an animal may all involve at once a symbolic, indexical and iconic relation.

The Multisensual Zoo

If the sign of an animal – or indeed of any other physical space at the zoo – involves a complex semeiotic such as I have just described, then further complexity is added by the fact that zoos are both "polysemeiotic" in the sense described *and* multisensual. But they are also multimodal (Kress and Van Leeuwen 1996) – semeiosis may occur by way of a variety of media.

We might begin by noting in this sense that, in addition to the animals themselves and to the geography of the displays, there are the actual signs. If it is true that zoos are in one sense all about the production of indexes – the displays are designed to "point" or draw the attention of visitors to the specimens, even as the specimens are brought to the zoo and made to "point to themselves" – they are also about the mediation of such indexes via the production of symbols. Each display has one or more "actual" signs that deploy one or more arguments explaining the nature of the nature on display. The relation between these signs and the animal-signs entails a complex process the analysis of which requires a delicacy of description beyond the scope of this essay. Here I will simply note that while such signs are themselves arguably "visual," their forms of realism and naturalism are not always those of environmental realism, or indeed of photographic naturalism. In many cases, diagrams and other highly schematic explanatory signs involve what is better described as a "rationalist" realism of natural history and the naturalism of the science textbooks and other representational genres of natural history that have been adapted, more or less successfully, to the pragmatics of zoo displays.[12]

To be sure, not all the signs (or sign-arguments) are visual or even mainly visual. Many zoos have developed displays that engage in what I described earlier as a "pedagogy of the senses." Such pedagogies usually entail a certain multimodality and multisensuality in their own right. On the one hand, actual signs with arguments are used to draw attention to – generate an index for – one or another sense. Such messages are, however, accompanied by a variety of *technologies of secondness*: displays expressly designed both to elicit and produce dynamics of action and reaction involving touch, smell, hearing and so forth. The most mechanical of these – in the full technical and discursive senses of the term – involve so-called interactive consoles. These encourage visitors – and children in particular – to press buttons or lift covers in order to obtain a more or less sensational sequence of action and reaction: to hear the call of a penguin, to test the speed of their own reaction when compared to that of other animals or to smell the scent of some plant or animal or its secretions.

Another form of multisensual secondness is found in the "affection sections" or petting zoos. In these visuality is combined with tactility, or with forms of display that constitute, in effect, haptic technologies: visitors (and again, especially children) are encouraged to feel sting rays in a tank, touch goats in a pen or perhaps stroke a blue-tongued skink in an "animal encounter" classroom or theater. While such encounters clearly involve what Peirce describes as energetic intepretants – an additional muscular or mental effort, a "further effect" in response to a sign – they are premised on an ideal of firstness insofar as they are designed to afford an encounter of the "first" kind, that is to say an immediate and unmediated interpretant, one that is not thought to be possible via the mass media. In the course of discussions with staff at Bristol, Paignton and other zoos, it became apparent the many zoo professionals assume that even if television ostensibly affords a greater naturalism by virtue of showing the animals in their actual habitats, zoos have a comparative advantage insofar as they allow visitors to experience the "real" animal. The Bristol Zoo slogan, for example, makes an explicitly sensualizing reference to this difference by suggesting that you can "See It–Sense It–Save It."

Earlier, I suggested that the design of many displays encourages the adoption of transmediating forms of visual observation. But the topography of some displays also encourages a somewhat more subtle form of multisensuality. This especially by way of so-called "immersion" enclosures that cater to the "rest" of the senses. For example, after highlighting the importance of the visual sense,

Keith McClintock suggests that the design of the landscape should "[s]urround visitors in sound, build in temperature extremes, add smell and encourage touch" (McClintock 2005: 37). "Immersion" may thereby be theorized not only as an effort to reproduce the *spatiality* of an animal encounter in the wild but also to reproduce both the firstness and the secondness of its sensualities.

This form of naturalism may be contradicted by another form of representation in zoos that I will only mention in passing, and that builds on a much older tradition of zoo-keeping, one that is in some respects closer to the circus: the staging of animal shows. Such shows tend to be explicitly designed to elicit what I describe as a circuit of anthropomorphism and "cosmomorphism" (Lindahl Elliot 2006). In such shows, visitors are invited to "humanize" the animals insofar as the animals are given human names and are made to perform quasi-human practices – for example, the Paignton Zoo has a show in which a parrot finds an object that has been concealed and shuffled beneath three different cups. But visitors (especially children) are also encouraged to "animalize" themselves insofar as they are invited to make the sounds and movements of the animals. If I mention this practice here, it is to begin to recognize that it may be misleading to speak in the univocal terms of a single economy of multisensuality.

Revisiting the Zoo

This last point is underscored by an analysis of visitor responses to zoo displays. At an earlier point in this essay I suggested that my initial analysis bracketed the lived space of zoos, and I would now like to consider the multisensuality of zoos from the perspective of ethnographic research that I conducted over a two-year period at the Bristol and Paignton zoos, beginning in the autumn of 2002. The ethnographic research included participant observation with thirty-five family groups (131 subjects in total), in-depth follow-up discussions in the participating families' homes, as well as a questionnaire designed to investigate adult zoo-user preferences *vis-á-vis* different modalities of naturalism in zoo displays.

An account of the aims, methodology, context and full results of this research project are beyond the scope of this essay.[13] Here I would simply like to describe a variety of practices that may adumbrate aspects of visitors' appropriation of the display practices I have just described, and which develop the suggestion that at least partly different economies of multisensuality may exist within one same zoo.

I would like to begin by noting a phenomenon that in one sense seems rather obvious, but which acquires a particular significance as part of a critique of the analysis of "visual culture." I have explained that the newest zoo displays are premised on a form of naturalism that seeks to recreate at least some aspects of an animal's original habitat. One of the features of the spatiality of such displays is commonly an emphasis on larger displays; and/or the inclusion of landscape features that limit the visibility of the animal (foliage, a hilly topography etc.). From one perspective, these design practices appear to confirm a "visual culturalist" reading: the displays attempt to transmediate aspects of the spatiality of the photographic naturalism I mentioned earlier. But the opposite might well be argued: by generating displays in which the specimen can disappear, zoos contradict the discourse of total visibility associated with natural history documentaries and other wildlife genres.

The ethnographic research revealed a similar contradiction: while surveys and oral commentary during visits suggested that most families valued large, and "naturalistic" displays *in principle*, the children especially expressed frustration when an animal could either not be seen, or could only be seen at a distance. The animals needed to be visible, and they needed to be visible close up. At least for the younger children, the nature of the landscape did not matter as much as being close to the animals. The most memorable aspects of visits for many of the families, and indeed the aspects that received the most attention in terms of the duration of the families' observations, were those in which animals engaged in manifestly kinetic activities – we return to the notion of an "energetic interpretant" – close to the visitors.

It might of course be argued that both of these phenomena are themselves a confirmation, if any were needed, of the preeminence of "visual culture": animals must be totally visible, they must be visible in "close-up" and they must be moving. Again and again many of the younger children asked if specimens that remained stock still (for example, the West African Dwarf Crocodiles) were real, or "pretend."

But even if these practices *are* evidence of visual transmediation (this time on the part of the visitors), it might well be argued that they are also evidence of the significance of a proxemics, and a form of corporeality that cannot be *reduced* to visual transmediation. Here the manner in which the children related to barriers at both zoos is significant. As I noted earlier, contemporary zoo designers tend to favour the ostensive erasure of the visitor/visited boundary, and of the boundary between any given display and the rest of the zoo. In many displays, glass is used extensively as a "transparent" medium, and indeed design discourses frequently equate glass barriers with a greater naturalism. In the course of my research, it became clear that this conception was routinely contradicted by children who tried to climb over, press against, or hoist themselves up and over in order to look *past* glass barriers. This despite the fact that, in principle at least, the same view could be seen through the glass, as could be seen above it.

Why was the glass experienced as a strong barrier by the children? One hypothesis is that they wished to move beyond any barrier whatsoever, a point I will return to in a moment. Another is that glass

– especially in ceiling-to-floor "windows" – gets in the way of the firstness of what I describe as the *sense of proximity*. The notion of the sense of proximity involves being close in terms of physical distance to an animal on display. It also involves a more fully multisensual encounter: ideally, one might see, hear, smell the animal and perhaps even feel the vibrations caused by its motions. But I suggest that, in addition to these possibilities, what is at stake is, if not a different "sense" in its own right, then certainly a complex "multisense." The visitor *reacts* (secondness) to the *wonder* (thirdness) of being in the immediate presence (firstness) – we might say the immediacy – of the animal. This even as the proximity makes possible a more fully multisensual encounter – not least, one that makes possible a bodily reaction of the kind associated, for example, with *cutis anserina* or the pilomotor reflex. In effect, the proximity melds thirdness and secondness and firstness, frequently as part of an overarching narrative (thirdness) of proximity mobilized by the zoos' promotional literatures. Glass might well thwart such encounters by sacrificing non-visual forms of multisensuality in favor of extreme visual proximity. Of course, there are usually good reasons, from a zoo's point of view, for such a sacrifice, reasons that remind us of the materiality of nature, as defined by Soper: it is not possible to pet a tiger.

I would now like to consider another dimension of spatial practice that also involves a more-than-visual relation to the barriers. As I have noted, many of the children wanted to go beyond the barriers, even in instances in which they were relatively "transparent" barriers. But it was striking to note that whereas adults stood and looked, children tended to touch and "press into" the different kinds of barriers. Again, it might be argued that this was no more than an expression of their desire to come closer to the animals, a desire that might itself be explained in terms of the iconicity and indexicality of close-ups in wildlife photography. In the course of my research, it none the less became clear that children visiting both zoos circulated through the different spaces in ways that constantly sought manual and other bodily contact with a variety of surfaces. Pressing against barriers was as much a matter of a desire for proximity, as it was a form of knowing the world by way of the secondness of bodily actions and reactions. For example, for several of the children, walking along a passageway in the Bristol Zoo's Twilight World frequently involved running a hand along the walls of the display even as they gazed at the displays on the other side of the corridor. A sculpture of a dinosaur fixed to one of the walls in the Paignton Zoo's reptile house afforded an opportunity to trace the contours of the crested back with the hand even as the head was turned towards the jewel-box displays of snakes. It was as if the navigation of the different spaces always involved a more or less conscious *visual* indexicality, but also, what might be described as a relatively unselfconscious haptic iconicity: a topography, a geography, was "likened" with the hand. The two sensualities – visual/indexical and haptic/iconic – redirected the attention when, for example, some protuberance, some unexpected texture produced an inversion in this order: the protuberance acted as a tactile index that led the children to look down to see what had interrupted the traveling hand.

A similar dynamic occurred when a better handhold was necessary. Indeed, perhaps the most wonderful example of the unanticipated pedagogic results of the phenomenon I am considering involved situations in which children at the Paignton Zoo used the signage on low fences to lever themselves up for a better view of a display, and then discovered aspects of the signs when they looked down in order to get a better handhold.

The practices I have mentioned also frequently involved what I describe as transcorporation: a *collective* form of "bodily" observation that in many respects seems like the antithesis of the kind of de-corporealized, individualized (and indeed "indivisualized") observer described by Jonathan Crary (1990) in relation to the *camera obscura*, and which, despite significant changes beginning the nineteenth century, arguably remains fundamental if not to modern culture then certainly to many forms of visual analysis. Almost all of the children liked to observe the animals while holding hands, hugging the parent's leg, or otherwise having some form of bodily contact with their parents or siblings. This was frequently such an automatic *modus observandi* that on several occasions I found myself being mistakenly hugged or taken by the hand by children who assumed for a moment that I was their parent. Even as they were absorbed visually by the piranhas or the monkeys, the green anaconda or the stick insects, the children reached out for physical contact with their parents, brothers or sisters. To be sure, walking the zoo, especially with the younger children, involved near constant demands to be lifted, carried or otherwise raised. In some cases this was a result of poorly designed displays that were too high to allow views for the youngest children. But in many other cases, it was also a matter of "comfort": of avoiding the walking, but also, of *being comforted* by what might well be described as the firstness of one's dad's or mum's body, the best possible "platform" from which to get a good look.

This form of collective observation was corresponded to by a more explicit form of distributed observation that involved the production of "pointed," and frequently of spoken, indexes. Visitors used the hand (or the index finger) to point out animals to each other, ran as a group to a different spot to get a better view, or worked together by lifting and in other cooperative means to better see this or that particular feature of a display. But perhaps more significantly, it also involved an on-going pedagogy that relied on what Peirce describes as dynamical interpretants: asking questions, "getting the attention" of another and directing it towards certain features of a display, and thereby partaking in the pleasure of eliciting the secondness of *a reaction* on the part of the daughter or the son, the brother or the sister, the mother or the father: "LOOOOOK!"

I would like to return now to the sense with which I began this essay: the sense of smell, but also, and somewhat more generally, to what can be described as the sense of "dirt." It is possible to describe this sense from the perspective of grotesque realism, and its concomitant naturalism and sensuality. I refer here to the work of Mikhail Bakhtin (1984) and its interpretation by Jesús Martín-Barbero (1993), in particular to their characterization of a realism for which:

> the ultimate and essential reality is the body-world and the world of the body," "a world view which gives value to what are commonly considered the lowest elements – the earth, the belly – posed in direct contrast to the higher things – the heavens and the human countenance" (Martín-Barbero 1993: 66).

Humor is an important aspect of this "world view," and as Martín-Barbero notes, its homonymy in the Spanish language with humor as a "visceral liquid" or bodily secretion is revealing. A significant dimension of the visits involved numerous jokes, especially but not only among the children and the working-class fathers about all things "humorous" in the double sense of the word. I have already commented on the reactions to strong odors. To this we might add the many occasions when the animal's excrements became the focus of attention: for example, at the Paignton Zoo one child beckoned us over to the howler monkey shelter to show us not a howler monkey – the monkeys were up in the enclosure's huge trees – but the poo that littered the floor of the shelter. If the animal shows organized by the zoos invited visitors to engage as spectators in what I described as the circuit of anthropomorphism and cosmorphism, then this was a kind of "lived" circuit of anthropomorphism: here were creatures doing in public everything that they ought to be doing in private, and this opened up all manner of possibilities for the exploration of social taboos such as defecating or indeed having sex in public. As one child put it, "Why is that beetle riding piggyback on the other beetle?"

Conclusion

In his critique of visual culture W.J.T. Mitchell suggests that "Visual culture entails a meditation on blindness, the invisible, the unseen, the unseeable and the overlooked" and that "it also compels attention to the tactile, the auditory, the haptic, and the phenomenon of synesthesia" (Mitchell 2002: 90). Insofar as this is the case, we should perhaps question whether the appellation "visual culture" is helpful, or if, on the contrary, it begins to close down analyses that, at least in contexts such as those constituted by the newest zoos, involve both more, and less, than visual culture.

In my own work, I have found it useful to articulate the visual aspects of zoo displays as part of a broader economy of multisensuality that both requires, but also makes possible multiple modalities of observation premised on varying forms of semeiosis, on varying degrees of corporealization (and indeed decorporealization) and changing criteria of realism and naturalism. I agree, in this sense, with Jonathan Crary (1990) when he says that it is necessary to substitute the emphasis on spectatorship and on passive conceptions of "seeing" with an understanding of the observer that regards him or her as one who sees, but in a more or less (de)corporealized way, within a prescribed set of possibilities, and in relation to conventions that are more than just representational practices. My own use of Peirce is nevertheless meant to offer a way of conceiving observation that deliberately both blurs, and redefines the opposition between so-called "representational" and "non-representational" practices.

With this account in mind, contemporary zoos' economies of multisensuality might well be described in terms of the juxtaposition, conflict or at times "symbiosis" of at least four different *modalities of observation*.[14] I describe the first of these modalities as the *iconic–environmental* mode, in which the predominant criteria of representation are derived from an environmental(ist) realism and from photographic/documentary naturalism. The visitor–observer is invited to observe the display in predominantly visual terms: the display should "look" like a particular environment, and of course the animals themselves constitute what Peirce describes as the phenomenon of "entelechy": the animal in the zoo is its own perfect representation, and the representation is its own perfect animal.

A second modality, which I have only briefly touched on in this essay, is what I describe as the *symbolic–scientific,* for which the predominant criteria of representation are derived from the rationalist criteria of realism associated with natural history and from the forms of naturalism found in biology, or more frequently in natural history textbooks as adapted more or less effectively to the pragmatics of zoo signage. The paradigmatic examples are the actual signs that explain the natural history of the animal, and/or some biological theory (e.g. evolution). The visitor–observer is invited to use verbal and other explanatory media such as diagrammatic signs to engage in a process of observation that in some respects inverts the order of representation assumed by iconic–environmental mode: what matters is not so much a high degree of visual iconicity, as an iconicity based on principles of explanatory abstraction, this in order to ascertain how and why the specimen on display is a likeness not just of itself, but of its *species*. Where this mode is based on more recent biological theories (as opposed to older natural history paradigm) the visitor–observer is invited to discern the hidden as well as the "universal" aspects of the specimen's and species' morphology and/or ethology.

A third modality of observation might be described as the *indexical–multisensual*, for which the predominant criteria of representation are derived from an empirical if not empiricist realism, the reality of the physical presence of the animals (and "their" landscapes) and from the naturalism associated with the instrumentalization of the sheer multisensuality of that presence. The paradigmatic example is the animal *encounter* or any activity at the zoo that involves the production of energetic interpretants afforded by touch, hearing, sound, proximity and so forth, for example the encounters afforded by the petting zoos. It is also enacted, however mechanically, by the "interactive" consoles that can frequently be found across zoos.

A fourth modality, which I describe as the *anthropomorphic–popular*, is premised on criteria of representation that are derived from a grotesque realism (Bakhtin 1984), and from forms of naturalism emerging from popular anthropomorphic and cosmomorphic performances. The paradigmatic example is an animal show in which animals are made to perform tricks that enable visitors to engage quite explicitly in the circuit of anthropomorphism and cosmomorphism. The animals are made to seem human, even as the humans are invited to animalize themselves. This mode of observation–participation might equally be described as a form of anti-naturalism; I nonetheless describe it as a type of naturalism because there is still a principle of iconicity or resemblance that is based on a conflation of the human and the non-human.

The following qualifications are required to clarify this typology, and its concomitant characterization of the economy of multisensuality in zoos:

First, and as my account of the last modality begins to suggest, the four modalities are by no means mutually exclusive. While it is possible to identify some types or aspects of exhibits that are more strongly associated with each of these modes, it is also possible to suggest that any one display can involve all four modalities. For example, the most sophisticated "immersion" displays arguably have elements of all four modalities of observation. More generally, we can say that even if some forms of anthropomorphism are more explicit than others, any human representation of non-human nature is, by its very nature, "humanizing." If we were to fully abstract the different relations of re/presentation from particular discourses, we might further conclude that any display must ineluctably have elements of each of the following forms of observation: a dimension of iconicity; indexicality; symbolism or convention and reference back to the "human."

Second, there is no necessary continuity between the predominant mode on the level of the design of the displays and their appropriation by visitors: my account is premised on the notion that different visitors might respond to any display on the basis of forms of observation that contradict or interrupt the intentions of zoo designers, or what the analyst might well regard as a given display's primary or "preferred" mode of observation. This begins to explain how it was that, for example, children responded with dynamic, and energetic interpretants to signs that otherwise called for what Peirce describes, somewhat ponderously, as "final logical interpretants," i.e. the sedimented wisdom of zoological and natural history discourses.

Third, at any given moment, an animal's actions may entirely transform the mode of observation and give rise to a different ascription of naturalism among visitors. For example, a gorilla charging up to a glass screen and pounding on it would almost certainly transform a mode premised on a predominantly iconic–environmental form of observation into one strongly driven by an indexical–multisensual mode.

The possibility of such transformations is at once the comparative sensual advantage of zoos – if all goes well, they are full of sensual surprises – and their fundamental dilemma: the animals might well be still or even invisible. If it is true that there is the possibility of more than one economy of multisensuality then it is also true that, in some situations, there might be no economy whatsoever.

Notes

1. Much of what I have to say in the following pages applies not just to zoos but to nature theme parks, safari parks and, despite their obvious differences, aquariums.
2. The research, titled *The New Zoos: Science, Media & Culture*, was funded by the UK's Economic and Social Research Council and formed part of its "Science in Society" program.
3. I am grateful to Simon Garrett, Education Manager at the Bristol Zoo Gardens, for alerting me to this example.
4. See, for example, Evans and Hall 1999; Mirzoeff 2002; Sturken and Cartwright 2001 or Walker and Chaplin 1997.
5. See Macnaghten and Urry (1998), or Lindahl Elliot (2006).
6. As suggested by Kress and Van Leeuwen, every realism has its naturalism:

   > realism is a definition of what counts as real, a set of criteria for the real, and it will find its expression in the "right," the best, the (most) "natural" form of representing that kind of reality, be it a photograph or a diagram (Kress and Van Leeuwen 1996: 163).

7. See Tarpy 1993 and Nichols 1996.
8. For an analysis of this form of naturalism in natural history documentaries see Lindahl Elliot 2001.
9. With Terry Eagleton, I define culturalism as "the doctrine that everything in human affairs is a matter of culture" (Eagleton 2000: 91).
10. Of the variant spellings of the word, Peirce chose "semeiotic" (with an "e") rather than "semiotic," as employed by Saussure – and I shall do this too as it seems like a convenient way of signaling that I employ an approach that is quite different from the Saussurean, or indeed post-Saussurean. Saussure's linguistic culturalism tends to inform, however distantly, the work of many cultural theorists and makes it difficult to conceive what Peirce described as an ideal–realist metaphysics – a metaphysics that

sought to move away from the dualism of the constructivist–naturalist dichotomy by way of a pragmatist philosophy.
11. In Peirce's theory, symbols are phenomenologically closer to thirdness while indexes are closer to secondness and icons to firstness. Any given sign may be all three types of signs at once, and will always involve not just thirdness, but a "degree" of secondness and firstness. This is, of course, merely a sketch that uses just one of Peirce's three trichotomies of signs; mindful of its degree of specialization, I have not employed the rest of Peirce's semeiotic theory in this essay. For a comprehensive account of this and of the other trichotomies, see Peirce (1931-58) CP 2: 243-264; for an analysis employing the other trichotomies, see Lindahl Elliot 2006.
12. In some zoos such forms of representation are something of a vanishing species, usually as a result of a critique of their didactic "voice," a voice that is associated with the older generations of zoos. Their continued presence in many zoos none the less attests to another feature that makes zoos rather more complex sites than my "visual culture" account has suggested: most zoos have a *mixture* of older and newer displays, and this in itself makes, if not for a certain multisensuality, then certainly for a certain heterogeneity of modes of observation. Especially, but not only, in European zoos it is common, for example, to find listed buildings more than a century old standing side by side with state of the art naturalistic/immersion exhibits.
13. While the research is clearly situated, my observations at other zoos and the presentation of the investigation's results to staff working in zoos beyond Bristol and Paignton suggest that it may be possible to generalize from its be findings to other UK zoos at least.
14. I presented a preliminary version of this model in a talk given at the 6th International Symposium of Zoo Design in Torquay, Devon, 2004; this talk has been included in the published symposium proceedings (see Lindahl Elliot 2005).

References

Bakhtin, M. 1984. *Rabelais and His World*. Purdue: Indiana University Press.

Beardsworth, A. and Bryman, A.E. 2001. "The Wild Animal in Late Modernity: The Case of the Disneyization of Zoos." *Tourist Studies*, 1(1): 83–104.

Crary, J. 1990. *Techniques of the Observer: On Vision and Modernity in the Nineteenth Century*. London: M.I.T. Press.

Davis, S. 1997. *Spectacular Nature: Corporate Culture and the Sea World Experience*. London: University of California Press.

Debord, G. [1967] 1995. *The Society of Spectacle*. Translated by D. Nicholson-Smith.

Douglas, M. [1966] 1991.*Purity and Danger: An Analysis of the Concepts of Pollution and Taboo*. London: Routledge.

Eagleton, T. 2000. *The Idea of Culture*. Oxford: Blackwell.

Evans, J. and Hall, S. (eds).1999. *Visual Culture: The Reader*. London: Sage with Open University Press.

Goddard, D. (ed.).1995. *Saving Wildlife: A Century of Conservation*. New York: Harry Abrahams.

Hanson, E. 2002. *Animal Attractions*. Princeton, NJ: Princeton University Press.

Houser, N. 1992. "Introduction." In N. Houser and C. Kloesel (eds) *The Essential Peirce: Selected Philosophical Writings, Volume 1*. Bloomington: Indiana University Press.

Hyson, J. 2000. "Jungles of Eden: The Design of American Zoos." In M. Conan (ed.), *Environmentalism and Landscape Architecture*. Washington, DC: Dumberton Oaks.

Kress, G. and Van Leeuwen, T. 1996. *Reading Images*. London: Routledge.

Lefebvre, H. 1991. *The Social Production of Space*. Oxford: Blackwell.

Lindahl Elliot, N. 2001. "Signs of Anthropomorphism: The Case of Natural History Documentaries." *Social Semiotics*, 11(3): 289–305.

—— 2005. "The Natures of Naturalistic Enclosures." In A.B. Plowman and S.J. Tonge (eds), *Innovation or Replication: Proceedings of the 6th International Symposium on Zoo Design*. Paignton: Whitley Wildlife Conservation Trust.

—— 2006. *Mediating Nature: Environmentalism and Modern Culture*. London: Routledge.

—— 2007. *Zoos in Modern Culture*. Cambridge: Polity (forthcoming).

Macnaghten, P. and Urry, J. 1998. *Contested Natures*. London: Sage.

Malmberg, M. 1998. *The Making of Disney's Animal Kingdom*. New York: Hyperion.

Martín-Barbero, J. 1993. *Communication, Culture, and Hegemony*. London: Sage.

McClintock, K. 2005. "Constructed Realism: Incorporating the Principles of Art and Perception to Communicate Realistic Natural Habitat." In A.B. Plowman and S.J. Tonge (eds), *Innovation or Replication: Proceedings of the 6th International Symposium on Zoo Design*. Paignton: Whitley Wildlife Conservation Trust.

Melfi, V. Browkett, A., Plowman, A. and Pullen, K. 2005. "Do Zoo Designers Know Enough about Animals?" In A.B. Plowman and S.J. Tonge (eds), *Innovation or Replication: Proceedings of the 6th International Symposium on Zoo Design*. Paignton: Whitley Wildlife Conservation Trust.

Mirzoeff, N. (ed.). 2002. *The Visual Culture Reader*, 2nd edn. London: Routledge.

Mitchell, W.J.T. 2002. "Showing Seeing: A Critique of Visual Culture." In N. Mirzoeff (ed.), *The Visual Culture Reader*, 2nd edn. London: Routledge.

Nichols, M. 1996. *Keepers of the Kingdom: The New American Zoo*. Charlotesville, VA: Thomasson, Grant & Lickle

Peirce, C.S. 1931–58. *Collected Papers*, 8 vols. Cambridge, MA: Harvard University Press.

—— 1992. *The Essential Peirce: Selected Philosophical Writings Volume 1*. Edited by N. Houser and C. Kloesel. Bloomington: Indiana University Press.

—— 1998. *The Essential Peirce: Selected Philosophical Writings Volume 2*. Edited by the Peirce Edition Project. Bloomington: Indiana University Press.

Rogoff, I. 2002 "Studying Visual Culture." In N. Mirzoeff (ed.), *The Visual Culture Reader*. 2nd edn. London: Routledge.

Saussure, F. de 1983. *Course in General Linguistics*. Translated by Roy Harris. London: Duckworth.

Shepherdson, D.J. 1998. "Introduction." In D.J. Shepherdson, J.D. Mellen and M. Hutchins (eds), *Second Nature: Environmental Enrichment for Captive Animals*. London: Smithsonian Institution Press.

Soper, K. 1995. *What is Nature?* Oxford: Oxford University Press.

Sturken, M. and Cartwright, L. 2001. *Practices of Looking: An Introduction to Visual Culture.* Oxford: Oxford University Press.

Tarpy, C. 1993. "New Zoos – Taking Down the Bars." *National Geographic*, 184(1): 2–37.

Walker, J.A. and Chaplin, S. 1997. *Visual Culture: An Introduction*. Manchester: Manchester University Press.

Seeing with the Hands, Touching with the Eyes: Vision, Touch and the Enlightenment Spatial Imaginary

Mark Paterson

Mark Paterson is a lecturer in Philosophy and Cultural Studies at the University of the West of England, Bristol. Along with articles on the senses and technology, he has recently completed a book for Routledge, *Consumption and Everyday Life* (2005). Currently he is writing a book for Berg, *The Senses of Touch*.
Mark.Paterson@uwe.ac.uk

ABSTRACT   Blindness has been a topic of great interest for philosophers, and the centrality of the so-called Molyneux problem explicitly raises questions concerning visual and tactile experience of the blind. Begun as a purely speculative philosophical exercise before ophthalmic operations could be performed, the debate continues and is examined here in relation to current work in psychology and neuropsychology. From debates and correspondence in the seventeenth century onwards, sparked by this hypothetical question, first-person accounts of the blind were sought to bolster the philosophical speculations. The question asked by

Molyneux is crucial in Enlightenment philosophy, and is discussed in a series of dialogs between philosophers such as Locke, Berkeley, Descartes and especially Diderot. This paper shows how a philosophical debate rooted in a distinct period in history has continued to excite the attention of those who attempt to draw together a psychological philosophy of sensory-spatial experience. In particular, the Molyneux problem concentrated on the interaction of the visual and the tactile, of hands and eyes, and how they are involved in spatial cognition. The legacy of these debates concerning the spatial imaginary of the blind remain pertinent to this day.

Introduction

In his famous *Letter on the Blind* of 1749, Denis Diderot writes of the experiences of a blind man in the French town of Puiseaux. Asked whether he would be overjoyed if he ever regained the use of his eyes, the blind man of Puiseaux supposedly replied

> I would just as soon have long arms: it seems to me that my hands would tell me more about what happens on the moon than you can find out with your eyes and your telescopes; and besides, eyes cease to see sooner than hands to touch. I would be as well off if I perfected the organ I possess, as if I obtained the organ which I am deprived of. (Diderot 1916: 77)

Knowing that the moon was far away and that the eye could gain no direct knowledge, this congenitally blind man asserts the necessity of touch as a more reliable path to knowledge, and analogizes the process of seeing with the eyes with that of touching with the hands. The blind man's testimony was used as empirical evidence in a long-running philosophical debate initiated by the so-called "Molyneux question," the answer revealing much about historical and contemporary attitudes to blindness, touch and space. What this debate and its hypothetical premise reveals, and why it captured the public imagination of the time, is a popular conception of the non-visual spatial experience of the blind, in other words a spatial imaginary. The spatial imaginary of the congenitally and adventitiously blind by the sighted remains of interest, as recent literature suggests (e.g. Gregory and Wallace 1963; Hull 1991; Kleege 1999; Sacks 2003). The urgency to validate this spatial imaginary through appeals to empirical evidence in the late seventeenth and early eighteenth centuries reveals the beginnings of a naïve phenomenological psychology.

We can identify two related strands of inquiry that characterize Enlightenment conceptions of blindness, both of which analogize hands and eyes, touch and vision, addressed in sections of this paper. Firstly, in the section "Hands and Eyes," the Molyneux question. William Molyneux's 1692 monograph *Dioptrica Nova* initially pitted his question concerning blindness, touch and vision couched in terms of hands and eyes, cubes and spheres: "If a man, blind from birth, suddenly gained vision, could he tell a sphere from a cube by sight alone on the basis of a lifetime of solely tactile experience?" (Riskin 2002: 23).[1] Although the question was initially put to British empiricist philosopher John Locke, the ensuing dialog drew contributions from Berkeley, Condillac and Diderot. The Molyneux problem was regarded by Ernst Cassirer in 1951 as *the* central question of eighteenth-century epistemology and psychology (in Gallagher 2005: 153). Secondly, in the section "Eyes and Hands," the related question of "what the blind see" (the subtitle of Sacks' 2003 essay) is addressed as an area of philosophical inquiry. In order to conceptualize the tactile imagery and spatial experience of the blind, Descartes and Diderot again consider the analogy between hands and eyes, touch and vision to be appropriate. Descartes describes the blind from birth as having the ability as it were to "see with their hands" (in Gregory 1967: 171). Further, how the congenitally blind (without any visual experience whatsoever) conceive of vision and the function of the eye, as revealed by the blind man of Puiseaux, deepens this analogy between eyes and hands.

In this paper we follow through Molyneux's hypothetical question, which predated available empirical data, and sample some subsequent discussions once the first cataract operations were performed. An assessment of the post-operative evidence is discussed in the section "Touching with the eyes." My concern is not simply to recapitulate previous discussions in philosophy (e.g. Morgan 1977; Eilan 1993) or experimental psychology (e.g. von Senden 1960; Jones 1975); Instead, I wish to investigate the long historical reach of a spatial imaginary that stretches from Descartes' *Dioptrique* (1637) to current concerns in psychology (e.g. Sacks 2003; Gallagher 2005), and my slant on this is threefold. Firstly, to make the assumption of an equivalence of the senses, substituting hands for eyes, touch for sight, is fundamentally to ask whether sensory perception is straightforwardly *cross-modal* (or *inter-modal*, sensory information being transferable from touch to vision) or actually *amodal* (sensory information being, prior to its processing as specifically audile, also visual, tactile etc.). Secondly, it shows how the Molyneux question remains unresolved to this day, despite the availability of post-operative evidence, and is addressed even in recent literature (e.g. Jacomuzzi et al. 2003; Gallagher 2005), albeit with modified terms of reference. And thirdly, it brings questions of relevance to modern technologies of sensory substitution systems, in thinking about the equivalence, or otherwise, of vision and touch, of "seeing with the hands" through electronic means. The fact is, as Josipovici observes, in thinking about blindness after Molyneux "we are all heirs of the seventeenth century" (1996: 69).

Hands and Eyes: Molyneux's Question

The philosophical problem of space and touch in the congenitally blind was raised by William Molyneux in a letter to John Locke after the publication of the first edition of Locke's *Essay Concerning Human Understanding* in 1690, before modern cataract operations could answer the question definitively. Berkeley, Diderot, Condillac and Voltaire subsequently became involved in a discussion of the philosophy of blindness. The letter, which concerned the hypothetical case of a man born blind who could now see, was reprinted in later editions of Locke's work, and became known in empiricist scholarship as "Molyneux's question." Locke posed the problem thus:

> Suppose a man born blind, and now adult, and taught by his touch to distinguish between a cube and a sphere of the same metal, and nighly of the same bigness, so as to tell, when he felt one and the other, which is the cube, which the sphere. Suppose then the cube and sphere placed on a table, and the blind man be made to see: *quaere*, whether *by his sight before he touched them*, he could now distinguish and tell which is the globe, which the cube? (1991: 67)

Remembering that the question was formulated before reliable cataract operations had been performed, the theoretical content of the question gauges whether the empirical content of the touch experience has a specificity of its own, or whether it can be equated *a priori* with the sensory experience of sight. Answering "yes" to the question therefore presumes "that our perceptions are amodal in their spatial content" according to Eilan (1993: 237), a position for which she claims there is much empirical evidence especially from child development studies, for example Piaget and Inhelder (1956; 1969). Conversely, answering "no" to Molyneux's question, as did Molyneux, Locke and Berkeley, is tantamount to arguing for the specificity of the senses, and what Eilan (1993: 240) describes as the "radical incommensurability" of the different sensory systems. Inter-modal (or cross-modal) perception, the translation from one sensory system to another, must be learned through repeated experience, a systematic perceptual correlation that commences at birth for the sighted, or after ophthalmic surgery, where possible, for the congenitally blind. Inter-modality seemingly requires that it be organized through an apprehending, unifying subject who transcends immediate sensory experience. Being an empiricist, Locke could allow no transcendence of the immediacy of experience and therefore sided with the incommensurability of the sensory systems. Molyneux's question and the issue of the specificity of the senses, especially touch and vision, is important for later theories of the psychology of blindness, and in particular the issue of spatial cognition in the blind. For von Senden in 1932 (1960), for example, what was felt by touch would produce a separate and differentiated series of sensory impressions from what was seen. The specificity of the sense modalities does not allow a higher-order integration of sensory information such that an abstract concept can be built up from different sense impressions. But this viewpoint has found support from Révész (1937; 1950) who claims that the distinct and independent modalities of visual, tactile and kinesthetic functions lead to separate and incommensurable spatialities for each. For Jones (1975: 467–70), echoing Berkeley's argument for the empirical association of the senses over time, vision is only one element in a mutually supportive system of the senses that becomes cemented through motility.

The problem is perhaps compounded by the fact that first-person historical accounts of visually impaired and blind subjects rarely speak of the specifically tactile experience of space, and those physicians involved have neither investigated nor problematized it rigorously. Early accounts of cataract operations also fail to make the crucial distinction between congenital and adventitious blindness, relative sensitivities to light, or even differing capacities for learning (e.g. von Senden 1960: 220; Monbeck 1973: 91; Gallagher 2005: 168). Molyneux's question therefore stands as a challenge to the scientific and physiological knowledge of the time, eliciting selective empirical testimony to a philosophical problem, and – through discussions of space, touch and sight – interprets it as a key issue in the debate between innate ideas and sensory experience.

In 1709, Berkeley provided a new twist to the debate, arguing for the specificity of the modalities of touch and sight, and denoting a stark separation between the senses. In asserting that there are no "general ideas" that stand outside immediate experience he agrees with Locke, but goes so far as to deny that space is visual at all. For Berkeley's *New Theory of Vision*, spatial experience was predominantly a tactile phenomenon:

> A man born blind, being made to see, would, at first, have no idea of distance by sight... The objects intromitted by sights would seem to him (as in truth they are) no other than a new set of thoughts or sensations, each whereof is as near to him as the perceptions of pain or pleasure, or the inward passions of the soul. (1983: 19)

In such a view there is no conflict between visual and tactile space, since for Berkeley there simply is no visual space. Additionally it means there is no space common to all the senses, no "general idea" or innate concept of space, as Morgan explains (1977: 179). As one of the fundamental premises of Berkeley's empiricism, therefore, space is not visual but haptic. Yet he concedes the possibility of amodal perception of sorts, speaking of "the extension and figure of a body, being let into the mind two ways, and that indifferently, either by sight or touch" (1983: lxviii). It is from this form of empiricism that Hume later argues in *A Treatise of Human Nature* of 1739 (1978) that the notion of the spatial extension of objects is derived from the association of experiences of touch and sight. The array of light on the retina for example, in and of itself, has no inherent meaning. Echoing Berkeley's sentiment, psychologists Warren and Rossano have more recently stated: "The observer learns to attribute meaning through the visual array[,] through the establishment of associations between patterns of visual stimulation and patterns of tactile and motor experience" (1991: 128). In other words, instead of the empirical view of Berkeley that "touch teaches vision," Warren and Rossano update this in terms of developmental psychology to say that "tactile/motor experience 'calibrates' visual experience" (1991: 128). This is supported by some psychological studies of touch in early infant development (e.g. Piaget and Inhelder 1956 and 1969; Jones 1975; Warren 1982; Millar 1994; Rose 1994; and neonates in Gallagher 2005). So far we have acknowledged the spatial character of tactile perceptions in philosophical debate. In inter-modal perception there are no actual equivalences between sensory data, say between hand and eye. Through associations of sensations and perceptual experience, however, a single, coherent perceptual content can occur so that familiarity with the *look* and *feel* of an object will make its subsequent recognition, through whichever sense modality, easier. The empiricist legacy continues from Molyneux through to recent developmental psychology (e.g. Gallagher 2005 as above), in which spatial cognition is constituted by both tactile-kinesthetic and visual experience. So far, this discussion has been predominantly couched in philosophical terms. But what difference does the empirical evidence actually make?

Touching with the Eyes: Cheselden's Patient

At the time Molyneux's question was posed in 1690 little empirical evidence on the subject existed mainly due to the fact that cataract operations were not routine. Although von Senden makes brief reference to an operation in the eleventh century, more detailed reports start to appear with a celebrated set of experiments on youths with cataracts by Cheselden (1728). Voltaire introduced a French readership initially to Cheselden's case study in his *Elements of Newton's Philosophy*, published in 1738 (1992). The debate was then taken up in France, being subsequently discussed by Diderot (1749/1916), Buffon (1749, in Morgan 1977: 16), and Condillac (1754/1930).

These ongoing discussions initiated by Molyneux's question were part of a larger Enlightenment fascination with the link between the senses and cognition (Barasch 2001: 149), in a climate in which musing on experiences of blindness and visual impairment were the topic of conversation in fashionable salons. In the words of Anagnos, neither Diderot nor anyone else "went beyond the boundaries of abstract psychological speculation" (in Farrell 1956: 18), and these questions would have remained hypothetical, both for philosophers and public alike, were it not for the historic surgical operations performed by William Cheselden in 1728. When Cheselden's patient saw for the first time, in 1728, he is also quoted as performing an equivalence between hands and eyes. Supposedly misconceiving space and distance, he initially collapses the distance between the object and its retinal impression, saying that visual objects "touch" the eye (in von Senden 1960: 219). In it he comments on the difficulties that Cheselden's patient had with the new-found visual world:

City Noise: the report of the commission appointed by Dr. Shirley W. Wynne, Commissioner of Health, to study noise in New York city and to develop means of abating it. From the CCA exhibition *Sense of the City/Sensations Urbaines* Collection Centre Canadien d'Architecture/Canadian Centre for Architecture, Montréal

> For a long time he distinguished neither magnitude, distance, situation, nor even figure... Everything he saw seemed at first to be upon his eyes, and to touch them, as the objects of the sense of feeling touch the skin. (in Morgan 1977: 23–4)

More crucially as regards Molyneux's question, Cheselden's patient was unable to distinguish with his sight what, with the help of his hands, he had been able to distinguish through touch. Whether cube or sphere, whether above or below him, his sight neither allowed him to recognize these objects nor their relative position in space. Perspective and distance were similarly problematic. Reportedly, when examining a painting he had to reach out and touch the surface to confirm there was only a two-dimensional representation, rather than there being three-dimensional solid bodies. Voltaire was surprised in his report of the blind man that "He asked which of the senses deceived him, that of feeling, or that of seeing" (1967: 65; also Diderot in Morgan 1977: 52).

Writing explicitly about the Molyneux problem, but with the benefit of Cheselden's report, in his *Letter on the Blind* of 1749 Diderot theorizes a relation between touch and space such that touch aids and informs the eye:

> It has to be agreed that we must perceive in objects an infinite number of things that the infant or the blind-born [given sight] do not perceive at all, even though such objects be painted upon the back of their eyes the same as ours; that it is not enough for objects to strike us, that we still must be attentive to their impressions; that as a consequence *we see nothing* the first time we use our eyes ... that experience alone teaches us to *compare* sensations with what occasions them; that since sensations have nothing that resembles objects essentially, experience has to construct about us analogies that seem to be purely conventional: in a word, it cannot be doubted that *touch serves a great deal to give the eye precise knowledge of the conformity between an object and the representation of it that the eye receives*. (in Creech 1996: 119, my emphasis)

In this Diderot finds agreement with Berkeley's speculation. In his questioning of the blind man of Puiseaux, Diderot assumes there is a spatial component to tactile experience, and that such tactile experience informs the eye. However neat a solution, the publication of Diderot's *Letter* is questioned by later findings. Platner in 1785 casts doubt on the veracity of Diderot's empirical information. Against Diderot's deduction that tactile experience is inherently spatial, Platner concludes, after investigation, that the congenitally blind literally have no awareness of space, and in the words of von Senden, that the sighted are simply "deceived by the verbal habits of the blind" when speaking of space, since they cannot share spatial understandings with the sighted (1960: 28).

After several hundred years of experimental evidence and surgical operations, should the question not be resolved? As Heller states, "the many studies of the restoration of sight do not provide unequivocal answers to Molyneux's question" (1991: 241). The answer is negative, therefore, for the following reasons. Firstly, it is a classic example of an attempt to gain privileged access to the contents of another person's mental state and cognitive processes, in this case of the blind by the sighted. However sophisticated the questioning, qualitative inquiry is hampered in this respect by the absolute inability to access another person's thought processes, and this problem persists in current examinations of experiences of blindness. There remain only fragments and imaginations. Secondly, there are complexities in the interpretation of the evidence over what counts as "blindness" and "sight," and in historical accounts these have not been systematized or standardized. Whether congenital or adventitious, and irrespective of the differing sensitivities to light that is a continuum from sighted to non-sighted, the historical evidence remains difficult to unpick as this information was not identified in the accounts. And thirdly, the post-operative experience varies greatly between patients, so that "learning how to see" (Gregory 1967; Sacks 1995) is different according to the plasticity and adaptability of each person and the level of previous retinal damage.

For example, von Senden in 1932 agrees with Platner's findings, arguing that tactile experience of the blind is entirely non-spatial, the blind person having no proper spatial representation of the objects touched. "What are features of shape to us are for him [sic] wholly unspatial, purely tactile distinctions of sensation or dynamic movement," he argues; "they are distinctions in the constancy of sequence and ordering of impressions" (1960: 49). Consequently he concludes there are no "absolute spatial concepts" for the blind, and that for the blind person there are only "relational concepts, ordered sequences and schemata" (1960: 61). This he infers from a selective reading of post-operative accounts. Descriptions of phenomena while sightless are related primarily to the peripersonal touch-space around the body, making it difficult to conceptualise a shape or figure lying beyond reach of hand or cane. Interviews conducted and published in a weekly newspaper with the congenitally blind subject Joan Getaz, questioned in 1928, further fueled the public imaginations of blind spatial experience. Without prior visual experience she conceptualized a tree serially and schematically as a temporal, textural sequence of trunk, branch and leaves. Owing to confusion over relative sizes compared with the body, Ms Getaz apparently assumed the tree was not much larger than a man. It was from his reading of these newspaper reports, as opposed to rigorous psychological treatments of case studies, that von Senden concluded that there is a difference between the visual and the tactile fields; the schema or ordered sequence is therefore not a "real consciousness of space" he maintains (1960: 69).

This view is not widely held. Recalling Berkeley's dogmatic assertion that our spatial knowledge comes primarily through touch, and that touch informs and appends vision, Warnock (in von Senden 1960: 322) and Jones (1975: 461) regard von Senden's view, that the congenitally blind have no spatial concepts, as equally dogmatic and unsupported by evidence. A more recent report examining tactile mapping suggests that the congenitally blind "may encode space in a serial, egocentric manner," a self-referential, route-type representation of space (Kitchin et al. 1997: 233). This perhaps encapsulates the contemporary, sighted imagination of the spatial cognition of the congenitally blind: the assumption of tactuo-spatial "images" or inner mental representations, especially of the static kind. After von Senden, one endeavour in more recent psychology is to escape these representational models, and from Gibson (1968) and Piaget and Inhelder (1971) onwards have stressed how spatial perceptions can occur without spatial "pictures" or inner mental representations, a spatiality resulting from active movement, informed by kinesthesia (Gibson 1950: 224; Karlsson and Magnusson 1994: 10 footnote 1). Indeed, Jones (1975: 466) argues specifically against what he calls the "visual map" theory, and asserts instead the importance of motor organization, citing empirical evidence for this. Returning to an insight by Diderot, when first opening our eyes we learn to compare sensations by experience, thereby admitting a *temporal* component to spatial perception. For cross-modal perception to occur for the Molyneux patient or for Diderot, there is a temporal aspect to sensory experience that forges associations between the sense modalities, thereby involving kinesthesia, the memory of touch-patterns, and other sensory-motor interventions. These observations would entail a modified answer to the Molyneux question, where what is commonly known as "visuo-spatial working memory" (Baddely 1992) relies on "mental images" in the blind that are neither specifically visual nor spatial, as Graven observes (2003: 102), and so memory allows the transfer of information between modalities. But at some level there is convergence between the sensory modalities, he argues, so that "a cognitive vision-touch link [is] derived from converging subsystems" (2003: 108). In terms of the absolute pragmatic experience of working memory, his evidence suggests that memory alone is not the intermediary of cross-modal transfer. Instead, there are underlying encoding processes at a "lower cognitive level" than memory (2003: 108), encoding experiences from different sensory subsystems. In other words, while memory might allow cross-modal transfer between modalities such as vision and touch, perception is more amodal than cross-modal. Where does this leave the experiences of eyes and hands, of blindness and spatial imagination?

Eyes and Hands: Diderot and Descartes

From the discussion of Molyneux and Locke in the section "Hands and eyes," we now consider Diderot's response to the post-operative evidence, which is more aligned with Descartes. Before Diderot nobody had elicited the testimony of blind subjects to contribute towards the Molyneux discussion, and so he stressed his subject was a real, not hypothetical person (in Morgan 1977: 32; Kennedy et al. 1992: 176). Diderot was convinced of the spatial character of tactile impressions in his subject, and questioned his subject about the spatiality of tactile impressions and the successive presence of the hand in different places. Compounded throughout history since the time of ancient Greece, we are familiar with a clear hierarchy of the senses in which vision was primary (Crary 1990; Jay 1994), and in which the absence of vision necessitated a substitute for sight. It is unsurprising that, in discussing the way the blind negotiate the world through the use of a stick, Descartes invoked a simplistic version of a hypothetical blind man in his *Dioptrique* of 1637:

> Without long practice this kind of sensation is rather confused and dim; but if you take men born blind, who have made use of such sensations all their life, you will find they feel things with such perfect exactness that one might say that *they see with their hands* (in Gregory 1967: 191, my emphasis).

The Cartesian concept of vision is therefore modeled after the sense of touch; the ability to "see with the hands" implicitly regards tactility as a lesser substitute for sight, even if it is the primary mode of spatial awareness and navigation for the blind. Such equivalence of sight and touch extends even to the idea of the fovea, the rodless part of the eye that affords the most acute vision. It is recognized that the most accurate part of our touch perception comes from the hands and especially the fingertips (e.g. Angell 1906: 147) because of the concentration of nerve endings in these regions. It is only natural to expect an analogy between the high definition optical discrepancy of the fovea and the highly discriminatory tactile sensing of the hands and fingertips. The accidental discovery in 1786 by Valentin Haüy that embossed script could be read by the fingers, for example, implied in the words of Farrell that "sensitive fingers ... could take the place of insensitive eyes" (1956: 93). The substitution of the sense of touch for the sense of sight, of hands for eyes, was therefore crucial in terms of the development of education for the blind.

Clearly Descartes' analogue between touch and vision, eyes and hands, is one of sensory poverty. Yet, unusually for the time, the same sensory analogue for Diderot instead proves the richness of the sensory world for the blind, and this fascinates him. This sensory analogue between the haptic and the optic persists in the education and psychology of the blind, and in 1930 Pierre Villey echoes the words of the blind man of Puiseaux, and similarly analogizes the neurophysiology of hands and eyes, or haptic foveation without color, implying the amodality of perception: "Sight is long-distance touch, with the sensation of colour added. Touch is near sight minus the sensation of colour, and with the sense of rugosity [texture] added. The two senses give us knowledge of the same order" (in Farrell 1956: 93). Even more recently, psychologists concerned with blindness have made the distinction between the near-space of haptic exploration and the far-space of locomotor exploration. Ungar (2000), for example, observes that "[i]n a sense, haptic exploration is like foveation without peripheral vision, in that the positions of objects not currently being attended to must be maintained in memory[,] and no cues are available to draw attention in any particular direction." Noting the use of "foveation" as a term of equivalence between sight and touch, in addition our attention is drawn to the distinction between the haptic (or prehensile) and locomotor explorations of space, of great importance for the congenitally blind. The reach-space of the hand and fingers is said to be "prehensile space," hence the foveation analogy, while "locomotor space" implies the movement of the entire body. Whether in immediate prehensile space or in the greater locomotor space afforded by movement, the notion of externality and the cognition of space for the blind is often performed and mediated through the hand and its prostheses, such as a cane or stick.

The same analogy concerning hands and eyes is extended to these prostheses, and finds expression once again in Diderot. Instead of the hypothetical unnamed blind man of Descartes' *Dioptrique*, the blind man of Puiseaux is asked directly how he conceives of the function and purpose of eyes. The answer confirms Descartes' interpretation of touch in terms of vision, as if there is an equivalence. "Madame," entreats Diderot,

> open the *Dioptrique* of Descartes, and you will find there the phenomena of vision related to those of touch, and illustrations full of men occupied in seeing with sticks. Neither Descartes nor those who have followed him have been able to get a clearer conception of vision (in Morgan 1977: 34).

Making the same analogy between the touch-space of the stick around the body and the visual field, the blind man of Puiseaux replies: "When I place my hand between your eyes and an object, my hand is present to you but the object is absent. The same thing happens when I reach for one thing with my stick and come across another" (in von Senden 1960: 64). Seeing with hands and seeing with the hands' prostheses afford different fidelities of touch, however. If foveation occurs within the fingertips, the hand and its prostheses are more peripheral and insensitive. In the same work, Diderot extends this foveation analogy:

> Should ever a philosopher, blind and deaf from birth, construct a man in the image of Descartes', I make bold to assure you, Madame, that he will place the soul in the fingertips, for it is from there that he receives all his sensations, all his knowledge (1977: 40; also de Fontenay 1982: 157–8).

Diderot acknowledges Descartes' view of the prosthesis and cane as an extension of perception, and in so doing accepts the observation that the sensorium is thereby extended. It is perhaps not the soul that is situated in the fingertips, as Diderot muses, but an acknowledgment that cognition is extended, literally reaching from brain to the peripersonal, prehensile space around the body. This reminds us of Kant's assertion that the hand is the "outer brain of man," heavily involved in spatial cognition (in Merleau-Ponty 1992: 316). Diderot therefore takes Descartes' encaphalous model of the senses, the sensorium being situated in the head or a set of internalized spatial representations, and makes it more acephalous or distributed. As Diderot argues, try telling the congenitally blind and deaf man that "the head is the seat of our thoughts," and he will report otherwise:

> the sensations he will have derived from touch will be, so to speak, the mold of all his ideas; and I would not be surprised if, after protracted meditation, he were to find his fingers as tired as we do our head (in de Fontenay 1982: 165).

Seeing with the hands, considering touch and sight as analogous (if not equivalent) in this way, is conceiving perception as amodal, disregarding the specificity of each of the senses in order to postulate some underlying correspondence. Hence the analogy between the hand, the stick and the eye in Descartes' *Dioptrique*, and for Diderot in *Letter on the Blind*. So far we have considered the way that "seeing with the hands" assumes the non-specificity of the senses. While the congenitally blind are able to make compensations and adjustments in terms of object recognition and spatial navigation, this does not mean that spatial perception is necessarily amodal or cross-modal *per se*. But, from his observations of the blind man's ability to recognize objects tactually, Descartes assumes in his *Dioptrique* that the capacity to form a whole representational framework is an innate property of the mind, not derived from the experiences or associations of the different senses.

Seeing with the Hands, Touching with the Eyes: Conclusion

Rather than it being rooted in any particular sense modality, then, Descartes thought of the process of constructing a spatial representational framework as amodal, independent of any specific sense modality (Jacobson et al. 1999). The argument for amodal spatial perception necessarily elides the specific perceptual content of the different sense modalities and has them contribute to an underlying, unifying faculty that makes sensations cohere at some cognitive level. Aristotle terms this capacity *aesthesis koine* or "common sensibility" in *De Anima* (424b–425a). As a result, for both Descartes and Diderot, "the senses are conceived more as adjuncts of a rational mind and less as physiological organs" as Crary puts it (1990: 60). As rational adjunct rather than distinct sensory modality, context and memory inflect the suitability of vision as an analogy to touch, or eyes to hands, and *vice versa*. If conceived as adjuncts in this way, the sometimes diverging and sometimes converging sensory subsystems dynamically inform and shape our perceptual experience of the world. Amodal spatial apprehension occurs as the result of just such a "unity of the senses" (Marks 1978), while the case of Cheselden's patient underlines the distinctness of newly-acquired sensory experience. The fundamental unity of the senses still holds currency in some circles, such as Carreiras and Cordina (1992). But, sagely enough, Diderot was actually arguing in the eighteenth century for something close to Graven's (2003) recent articulation of converging–diverging sensory subsystems, and in terms comparable to Gallagher's (2005) discussion of intermodal neonate vision. He was to hold a *correspondence* rather than an *equivalence* between the senses, while conceding the possibility that the senses have a specificity of their own: "It is easy to conceive that the use of one of the senses can be perfected and accelerated by the observations of another; but it is not easy to conceive that between their functions there is an essential dependence" (1916: 62). Presciently, this can be translated into the psychological idiom of amodal and cross-modal perception, where cross-modal perception equates with correspondence.

This debate, and speculation concerning intermodal and amodal perception, as we have seen, has been updated in recent neuropsychological writings. Space does not allow a complete survey or development of these ideas, but it is sufficient to note that the same debate concerning visualization and cognition between vision and touch persists. Indeed, the question of "visualization" in the blind, of what the blind "see," is addressed specifically as an indication of the brain's organization of sensory information as amodal and adaptable by Sacks (2003) and Motluk (2005). Such recent popular science articles about what the blind "see," with Sacks in the *New Yorker* interviewing a number of blind respondents, and Motluk in *New Scientist* profiling a blind artist, can be seen as a continuation of Diderot's attitude of inquiry. Sacks for example writes of mounting neuropsychological findings that reinforce Crary's view, above, that the senses are no longer distinct modalities, that the "sensory modalities can never be considered in isolation": "There is increasing evidence from neuroscience for the extraordinarily rich interconnectedness and interactions of the sensory areas of the brain, and the difficulty, therefore, of saying that anything is purely visual or purely auditory, or purely anything" (2003: 55). Relating this back to his case studies, and more usefully in the context of this paper's discussion of cross-modal (or intersensory, intermodal) perception as opposed to amodal (metamodal) perception, he then states: "The world of the blind, of the blinded, it seems, can be especially rich in such in-between states – the intersensory, the metamodal – states for which we have no common language" (2003: 55). Imaginations of the experience of blindness, from Descartes onwards, have furthered the substitutions of sensory experiences, of hands and eyes, as we have seen. These and other incidences of intersensory experience (or cross-modality) have implications for the synesthetic richness of experience in blind and sighted alike, which is an important area of inquiry in phenomenology ("synesthetic perception is the rule" argued Merleau-Ponty in 1945 [1992: 229]) and more recent psychology and cognitive science. And cross-modal transfer from vision to either audition or touch is the basis for technologies of sensory substitution systems for the blind and visually impaired, as investigated in the work of Karlsson (1996) and Kitchin et al. (1997), and exemplified by Bach-Y-Rita (in Morgan 1977).

Returning to the theme of eyes, hands and the spatial imaginary, it is fitting to state the full title of Diderot's essay: "Lettre sur les aveugles, á l'usage de ceux qui voient." The subtitle, translated as "for the benefit of those who see," is obviously intended as part of the Enlightenment fascination with the sensory world of the blind on the part of those who can see, arguably reducing a phenomenology of blindness into a speculative parlor game for the sighted, notwithstanding the assumption of an absolute distinction between "blind" and "sighted" experience that has been made more complex in the course of this paper. Yet, for another blind subject who underwent an operation to see in 1963, one phrase resounds, both in the psychological case study by Gregory and Wallace (1963) and in Sacks' report (1995). The blind subject, responding to his newly-discovered visual world, has difficulty identifying an object. Being led to that object, and able finally to touch it, he is able to correlate the visual blobs of color he sees with his eyes with what had been familiar in his previously tactile world, and he states: "Now that I've felt it, I can see!" (in Sacks 1995: 126).

Note

1. There are two alternative spellings that were not standardized at the time. "Molyneux" is sometimes spelt "Molineux" (e.g. in Monbeck, 1973) or the Latinized "Molinaeus" (in D'Alembert, 1772).

References

Angell, J. R. 1906. *Psychology: An Introductory Study of the Structure and Function of Human Consciousness*. New York: Henry Holt and Company.

Baddely, A. D. 1992. "Working Memory." *Science*, 255: 256–9.

Barasch, M. 2001. *Blindness: The History of a Mental Image in Western Thought*. London: Routledge.

Berkeley, G. 1983. *Philosophical Works including the Works on Vision*. London: Dent.

Carreiras, M. and Codina, B. 1992. "Spatial Cognition of the Blind and Sighted – Visual and Amodal Hypotheses." *Cahiers De Psychologie Cognitive-Current Psychology of Cognition*, 12(1): 51–78.

Cheselden, W. 1728. "An account of some observations made by a young gentleman, who was born blind, or lost his sight so early, that he had no Remembrance of ever having seen, and was couch'd between 13 and 14 years of age." *Philosophical Transactions of the Royal Society of London*, 35: 447–50.

Condillac, É. B. 1930. *Treatise on the Sensations*. Translated by G. Carr London: Favil.

Crary, J. 1990. *Techniques of the Observer: On Vision and Modernity in the Nineteenth Century*. London: MIT Press.

Creech, J. 1986. *Diderot: Thresholds of Representation*. Columbus: Ohio State University Press.

D'Alembert, J.L.R. 1772. "Blindness." In *Selected Essays from the Enclyopedy* Translator unknown. London: Samuel Leacroft.

de Fontenay, E. 1982. *Diderot: Reason and Resonance*. New York: George Braziller.

Diderot, D. 1916. *Diderot's Early Philosophical Works*. Chicago: The Open Court Publishing Co.

—— 1977. "Letter on the blind, for the benefit of those who see." Translated by M.J. Morgan, in M. J. Morgan, *Molyneux's Question: Vision, Touch and the Philosophy of Perception*. Cambridge: Cambridge University Press.

Eilan, N. 1993. "Molyneux's Question and the Idea of an External World." In *Spatial Representation: Problems in Philosophy and Psychology*. Edited by N. Eilan. Oxford: Blackwell.

Farrell, G. 1956. *The Story of Blindness*. Cambridge, MA: Harvard University Press.

Gallagher, S. 2005. *How The Body Shapes the Mind*. Oxford: Clarendon Press.

Gibson, J. J. 1950. *The Perception of the Visual World*. London: George Allen & Unwin.

—— 1968. *The Senses Considered as Perceptual Systems*. London: George Allen & Unwin.

Graven, T. 2003. "Aspects of Object Recognition: When Touch Replaces Vision as the Dominant Sense Modality." *Visual Impairment Research*, 5(2): 101–12

Gregory, R. L. 1967. *Eye and Brain: The Psychology of Seeing*. London: World University Library.

—— and Wallace, J. 1963. *Recovery from Early Blindness: A Case Study*. Experimental Psychology Society Monograph No. 2. Cambridge: Heffers

Heller, M. A. 1991. "Haptic Perception in Blind People." In M.A. Heller and W. Schiff (eds), *The Psychology of Touch*. London: Lawrence Erlbaum Associates.

Hull, J. M. 1991. *Touching the Rock: An Experience of Blindness*. London: Arrow Books.

Hume, D. 1978. *A Treatise of Human Nature*. 2nd edn. Oxford: Clarendon Press.

Jacomuzzi, A. C., Kobau, P. and Bruno, N. 2003. "Molyneux's question redux." *Phenomenology and the Cognitive Sciences*, 2: 255–80.

Jay, M. 1994. *Downcast Eyes: The Denigration of Vision in Twentieth-Century French Thought*. London: University of California Press.

Jones, B. 1975. "Spatial Perception in the Blind." *British Journal of Psychology*, 66(4): 461–72.

Josipovici, G. 1996. *Touch : An Essay*. London: Yale University Press.

Karlsson, G. 1996. "The Experience of Spatiality for Congenitally Blind People: A Phenomenological-Psychological Study." *Human Studies* 19(3): 303–30.

—— and Magnusson, A.-K. 1994. "A Phenomenological–Psychological Investigation of Blind People's Orientation and Mobility." Report 783 from Department of Psychology, Stockholm University: pp. 1–22.

Kennedy, J. M., Gabias, P. and Heller, M. A. 1992. "Space, Haptics and the Blind." *Geoforum*, 23(2): 175–89.

Kitchin, R. M., Blades, M. and Golledge, R. G. 1997. "Understanding Spatial Concepts at the Geographic Scale without the use of Vision." *Progress in Human Geography*, 21(2): 225–42.

Kleege, G. 1999. *Sight Unseen*. London: Yale University Press.

Locke, J. [1690] 1991. *An Essay Concerning Human Understanding* [Abridged] London: Everyman's Library.

Marks, L. E. 1978. *The Unity of the Senses: Interrelations among the Modalities*. London: Academic Press.

Merleau-Ponty, M. 1992. *The Phenomenology of Perception*. Translated by C. Smith. London: Routledge.

Millar, S. 1994. *Understanding and Representing Space: Theory and Evidence from Studies with Blind and Sighted Children*. Oxford: Oxford University Press.

Monbeck, M. E. 1973. *The Meaning of Blindness: Attitudes Towards Blindness and Blind People*. London: Indiana University Press.

Morgan, M. J. 1977. *Molyneux's Question: Vision, Touch and the Philosophy of Perception*. Cambridge: Cambridge University Press.

Motluk, A. 2005. "The art of seeing without sight." *New Scientist*, 2484 (January 29): 37.

Piaget, J. and Inhelder, B. 1956. *The Child's Conception of Space*. London: Routledge & Kegan Paul.

—— 1969. *The Psychology of the Child*. New York: Basic Books.

—— 1971. *Mental Imagery in the Child: A Study of the Development of Imaginal Representation*. New York: Basic Books.

Révész, G. 1937 "The Problem of Space with Particular Emphasis on Specific Sensory Spaces." *American Journal of Psychology*, 50.

Révész, G. 1950. *The Psychology and Art of the Blind*. London: Longmans Creen & Co. Ltd.

Riskin, J. 2002. *Science in the Age of Sensibility: The Sentimental Empiricists of the French Enlightenment*. London: University of Chicago Press.

Rose, S. A. 1994. "From Hand to Eye: Findings and Issues in Infant Cross-Modal Transfer." In D J Lewkowicz and R Lickliter (eds), *The Development of Intersensory Perception: Comparative Perspectives*. Hove: Lawrence Erlbaum Associates.

Sacks, O. 1995. *An Anthropologist on Mars: Seven Paradoxical Tales*. London: Picador.

—— "A Neurologist's Notebook: The Mind's Eye – What the Blind See." *New Yorker* (July 28), pp. 48–59.

Ungar, S. 2000 "Cognitive Mapping without Visual Experience." In R. K. S. Freundschuh (ed.), *Cognitive Mapping: Past, Present and Future*. London: Routledge.

Voltaire (1992) "Elements de philosophie de Newton." In *Oeuvres completes, vol. 15*. Oxford: Alden Press.

von Senden, M. 1960. *Space and Sight: The Perception of Space and Shape in the Congenitally Blind before and after Operation*. Translated by P. Heath. London: Methuen & Co.

Warren, D. H. 1982. "The Development of Haptic Perception." In W Schiff and E Foulke (eds), *Tactual Perception: A Sourcebook*. Cambridge: Cambridge University Press.

Warren, D. H. A. and Rossano, M. J. 1991. "Intermodality Relations: Vision and Touch." In M. A. Heller and W. Schiff (eds), *The Psychology of Touch*. London: Lawrence Erlbaum Associates.

SENSORY DESIGN

Sporting Sensation

John F. Sherry, Jr.

John Sherry, Herrick Professor of Marketing and Department Chair, Mendoza College of Business, University of Notre Dame, is an anthropologist who studies the sociocultural dimensions of consumption. He is a Fellow of the American Anthropological Association and the Society for Applied Anthropology. Sherry is a past President of the Association for Consumer Research and a former Associate Editor of the Journal of Consumer Research. jsherry@nd.edu

Over several years and several publications, my colleagues and I have explored the carnal kindergarten of ESPN Zone Chicago, the quintessential postmodern sports bar reprised as male preserve, where physical exertion and virtual exhaustion whipsaw the consumer from the intimate immediacy of playing field to the projective pixilation of telepresence, rocking the sensorium to its very roots

The retail theatrics of this spectacular shrine to America's civil religion, to which the faithful flock in search of the elixir of youth – the lived experience of play, served up Disney-style through the mediated screen of ESPN authenticity – produces an amazingly uniform response among its pilgrims: sensory overload. The Zone is a two-story sensory inundation tank,[1] in which immersed consumers are so bombarded with sensation they have labored mightily to co-create that they often exit the premises reeling, marveling at the spectacle-induced variant of phantom limb syndrome felt long after departure.

The threshold of this eatertainment venue is redolent of brew and pub grub and thrums with the beat of mixtape music pumped out onto the street, luring lookers into the Atrium. Once inside, the gaze is engaged by ubiquitous batteries of video monitors,[2] most larger than life, enticing viewers into the epicenter of sportsworld, by scoreboards and tickers and crawlers reminiscent of sports books, by luminous signage of corporate sponsors and, most of all, by fellow travelers on the gaming odyssey that makes every player a performer,[3] every spectator a participant. The glance caroms from monitor to arcade screen to ball court and back again, marking play and crowd in its sweep, accompanied all the while by a frenetic soundscape of electronic sportnoise and the cheers, jeers and commentary of patrons. Drawn ever upward to field and screen, the gaze gives way to a haphazard haptics of navigation, as consumers meander from Atrium to Arena to Throne Zone, brailling exhibits, tossing balls, breaking sweat[4] more often on the virtual skis, motorcycles, skeet and bowling than the "real" games, and bumping into one another in the crowded communitas of the play space, even as they try to avoid spilling their beer while washing down buffalo wings.

The sanctum sanctorum of the Zone, the Ultimate Viewing Area, is the promised land of the true sports fan,[5] a dream come true both figuratively and literally, where all the senses are enlisted in the service of an in-to-body experience of immanence. Ensconced in a luxurious leather La-Z Boy, enveloped in surround-sound audio feeds of dozens of live sports matches broadcast on a bank of enormous screens and controlled by a finger panel on the arm of the recliner, served by women who ensure constant delivery of food and drink, the rapt consumer may experience many a slip between cup and lip as the images wash over him, or as an eerily authentic crack of a bat and the reflexive expectation of a line drive to the head startles him from reverie.[6] The experience of the Throne is the apotheosis of the Zone's tagline challenge to the consumer: "Eat. Drink. Watch. Play. What More Could You Want?"[7] Provision of the staff of life, couched in

Ice palace of 1889 as it was intended to be. From the exhibition *Sense of the City/ Sensations Urbaines*. Gift of the Hon. Serge Joyal, p.c., o.c. Collection Centre Canadien d'Architecture/ Canadian Centre for Architecutre, Montréal

the imperative, clinched in the rhetorical, delivered while you're sitting down. The good news and the bad news is just that simple.

In this intriguingly imagineered reverse panopticon,[8] synesthetic sensation (the tactile dimension of vision, the visual quality of sound, the aural reverberation of smell) shapes experience in highly nuanced fashion for individual consumers. Sweat cuts cologne and returns someone to the echo of the locker room. Pebbled texture of a ball viewed in flight returns another to the leaden feel of a critical charity stripe. Butt on recliner returns some to home, and others to Momma. Intersense modalities magnify the impact of the built environment on consumer experience. Consumers leave the Zone while in the zone, both energized and enervated, buzzing and buzzed.

As themed flagship brand stores move beyond their 3-D advertising origins to become the emplaced brandscapes that ground our experience economy, a telematic aesthetic increasingly engages our senses. The artifactual and the electronic fuse in a way that permits the site to inhabit us. Understanding the sensual circuitry of this fusion is an exciting challenge for twenty-first century social science.

Notes

1. To borrow a phrase from Stephen Colbert, whose notion of "truthiness" is so in sync with the entertainment economy ethos that spawns such themed flagship brand stores.
2. Yes, even in bathrooms, where collegiate fightsongs provide an urgent aural aide de toilette.
3. Even those overserved patrons in overstuffed easy chairs asleep in the Screening Room.
4. Visceral feelings of motion(-sickness) are widely reported for arcade games.
5. Etymologically, "fan" and "fanatic" are cousins with the same liturgical roots.
6. Pick your favorite Freudian regression – phallic or uterine – and find it represented in our informants' fantasies.
7. The answer, of course, is not "Sex" (which abounds here in heterosexual fantasy, homoerotic sublimation and general carnal sensuosity), but, simply, "More."
8. Managers watch you watch them watch you while you watch others watch you watch them...

References

Kozinets, Robert V., John F. Sherry, Jr., Benét DeBerry-Spence, Adam Duhachek, Krittinee Nuttavuthisit and Diana Storm. 2002. "Themed Flagship Brand Stores in the New Millennium: Theory, Practice, Prospects." *Journal of Retailing*, 78 (1): 17–29.

Kozinets, Robert V., John F. Sherry, Jr., Diana Storm, Adam Duhachek, Krittinee Nuttavuthisit, and Benét DeBerry-Spence. 2004. "Ludic Agency and Retail Spectacle." *Journal of Consumer Research*, 31 (3): 658–72.

Sherry, John F. Jr., Robert V. Kozinets, Diana Storm, Adam Duhachek, Krittinee Nuttavuthisit, and Benét DeBerry-Spence. 2001. "Being in the Zone: Staging Retail Theater at ESPN Zone Chicago." *Journal of Contemporary Ethnography*, 30(4): 465–510.

Sherry, John F. Jr., Robert V. Kozinets, Diana Storm, Adam Duhachek, Krittinee Nuttavuthisit and Benét DeBerry-Spence. 2003. "Gendered Behavior in a Male Preserve: Role Playing at ESPN Zone Chicago." *Journal of Consumer Psychology*, 14(192): 151–8.

Mind and Memory: The Blessed Sacrament Chapel, Church of St Ignatius[1]

Ruth Coates

Ruth Coates, M.Arch, is an architect for The Miller|Hull Partnership, LLP in Seattle. She was the recipient of the University of Illinois at Urbana-Champaign's Ryerson Traveling Fellowship, which provided a four-month study of ritual paths around the world.
rcoates@millerhull.com

A glowing alcove at the Church of St Ignatius, the Blessed Sacrament Chapel is a space steeped in sensory detail. Tall and cylindrical, it is a small retreat for ritual and prayer, and acts as a spiritual core for the building. In fact, it takes an important position in the building's dialog between modern construction and ancient archetypes. What the mind observes at the chapel is added to by what the body feels, creating a rich and multi-layered experience.

The chapel – a roughly eight-foot square room – is visible from the entry of the church. Diffuse light glances off the curved and tilted surfaces and gives the room a warm and glowing quality in contrast with the dim interior of the sanctuary. Thick walls and translucent windows obscure the surrounding campus and muffle distractions. Immediately there is a separation from the outside world. Once inside, the room's small scale creates an awareness of one's bodily presence. Unlike when entering a large, spacious room, it is impossible here to ignore the presence of walls, objects and textures. This forced proximity gives a visitor close contact with the level of detail that would have been lost in the expanse of a bigger space. One notices that the plaster walls are not factory formed: they bear unmistakable traces of the human hand. A beeswax coating demonstrates the passage of time with hardened drips and runs evident on the surface of the wall. How long has the candle been burning in this room, one might wonder – or is the room itself the candle? Inscriptions engraved into the walls are taken from various spiritual guides throughout history, recalling the timelessness of religion. Lastly, a tree sculpture entitled *Faith,* by Linda Beaumont, anchors the space. A tabernacle candle is hung from its branches. This is one of the most profound gestures within the building, symbolizing the struggle of life, eternal growth or nature's shelter. The expression of the tree sculpture is incredibly literal – being an actual dried madrona tree – and seems to contradict the abstract nature of the building. Yet the presence of such a timeless metaphor does imbue the room with an intensity of meaning. Despite these elements, which conjure ancient imagery, the chapel does lack the smells that are often steeped into aged buildings: candle smoke, incense, damp stone and cool mustiness. One might argue that these more subtle sensory perceptions give legitimacy to historical symbols in a way that can't be recreated in a modern building. Perhaps it is a less vivid place because of that, but it is the contemporary norm.

The chapel's greatest asset, and its greatest fault, is its situation within the building. It occupies a very prominent spot in the entry sequence of the building. Visible from the narthex it is seen on axis as visitors enter the sanctuary and find their seats for mass. This does allow the patron to have a glimpse of the space and feel invited by its glow. It also makes it a very significant part of the interior composition.

However, this same emphasis detracts from the privacy that its use calls for. Places of sacrament, ritual and meditation often benefit from a sense of privacy that allows deeper thought to take place. While the material construction of the chapel has succeeded in sheltering the user from the commotions and disturbances of the world outside, the design has failed to provide seclusion from the body of the church; users of the chapel are able to see the front door and the entire sanctuary, providing unavoidable distractions.

At the same time, occupants are not necessarily visible from the sanctuary. This means that because of the intimate scale of the room, it is impossible to enter or even just peek in without disturbing an occupant. Comparisons with the chapel of Ronchamp by Corbusier are obvious, but important regarding the articulation of these small alcoves. In Corbusier's small prayer rooms, one approaches from the rear, and so avoids disturbing any occupants.

Taken as a part of the overall design of St Ignatius, the chapel is a thoughtful complement to the larger whole. Its location, metaphorical

Figure 1
Entry to the Blessed Sacrament Chapel, Church of St. Ignatius, Seattle.
© 2005 Ruth Coates

gestures and detail contribute to the essence of the church. Its interior feels handcrafted and slightly primitive as do the sanctuary and narthex. The roughly plastered walls form a continuous surface joining the church and chapel. This technique allows the flowing ceilings and walls to undulate seamlessly and suggest more ancient churches.

This dialog between past and present is evident throughout the project. Elements made possible with modern construction such as large expanses of glass with butt-glazed corners, tilt-up concrete and longer spans contrast with interior treatments that take the mind back several centuries. It is an awareness that the architect, Steven Holl has strived to give visitors from the moment they enter the chapel by pulling on the handcrafted bronze door pulls. Forged by hand they

Figure 2
View upward. The Blessed Sacrament Chapel.
© 2005 Ruth Coates

are irregular in shape yet very smooth as if centuries of people had passed through this portal. In addition, dripping candle wax, a dim sanctuary, hand-troweled plaster and thick glass windows call to our instincts and our past. These symbols of memory activate our feelings and our body's experience. At the same time, texture, changing light and muffled sound within the human scale of the chamber offer something observable to the senses. All these components acting together allow the chapel to linger in the mind *and* the body.

It is perhaps this attention to sensory design that is most successful about the Blessed Sacrament Chapel. It proposes that a multilayered awareness heightens the spiritual moment. Engaging one's consciousness on varied levels forms a stronger platform for meditation and deeper thought. Maybe this is why, throughout time, sacred buildings have incorporated multi-sensory elements to recall rituals, elicit emotions and create community. Thoughtfully placed light and shadow, soaring vaults and narrow passages, incense and lit candles, religious symbols and artifacts are timeless examples that people of many ages and cultures can relate to with similar responses. In this respect, the Blessed Sacrament Chapel is an important building not only for our time – making use of modern capabilities – but as continuation of human memory with experiences that bind us to our past.

Note

1. The Church of St Ignatius is part of the campus of Seattle University.

Cultural Politics

Edited by John Armitage, University of Northumbria,
Douglas Kellner, University of California, Los Angeles and
Ryan Bishop, National University of Singapore.

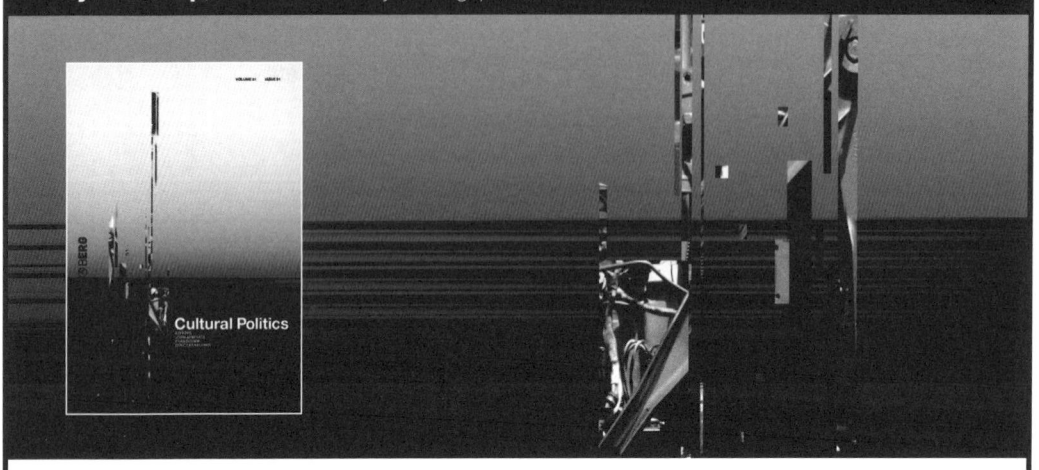

***Cultural Politics* explores precisely what is cultural about politics and what is political about culture.**

Cultural Politics publishes work that analyses how cultural identities, agencies and actors, political issues and conflicts, and global media are linked, characterized, examined and resolved.

While embodying the interdisciplinary and discursive critical spirit of contemporary cultural studies, this journal also emphasizes how cultural theories and practices intersect with and elucidate analyses of political power.

Board members include:
Jean Baudrillard, Paul Virilio, Gayatri Chakravorty Spivak, Les Back, Nigel Thrift and Chua Beng Huat.

Indexed by:
IBSS (International Bibliography of Social Sciences), SocINDEX (Ebsco) British Humanities Index, Sociological Abstracts and Political Science Abstracts (CSA).

Published 3 times a year in March, July and November.

ISSN: 1743-2197	Individual	Institutional
1-year subscription 2006	£40/$75	£155/$279

BERG

Order online at www.bergpublishers.com or call +44(0)1767 604951
Institutional subscriptions include online access through www.IngentaConnect.com
To order a sample copy please contact enquiry@bergpublishers.com
View issue 1.1 free online at www.ingentaconnect.com

Architecture of the Immediate: Steven Holl's Addition to the Cranbrook Institute of Science

Stephen Temple

Stephen Temple is Assistant Professor at the College of Architecture, University of Texas San Antonio. BArch: Carnegie Mellon University; MS Architecture: University of Texas at Austin. He has taught in design and architecture since 1994, following fourteen years as a practicing architect. His research is in design criticism and philosophy, phenomenology and architectural education, especially basic design education. stemple@utsa.edu

The architecture of Steven Holl is developed as a catalyst to perceptual experience, precisely to engage a sensitized consciousness in search of the profound in architectural experience. Holl believes that, because we are born into the world of physical objects, in the living of our lives we are naturally able to fully experience the perceptual phenomena of our surroundings and, thus, have joy in the immediacy of our sensory perceptions. Inspired by the phenomenology of Maurice Merleau-Ponty, Holl designs architectural experience as an interplay between the concrete immediacy in our perception of the physical world and its abstraction as mental construct, thus offering a simultaneity of physical being and mental life as a profound transformation of everyday experience. Holl develops architecture as an intensification of a particular cast of mind, stating that:

Stephen Temple

> The experience of space, light and material as well as the socially condensing forces of architecture are the fruit of a developed idea. When the intellectual realm, the realm of ideas, is in balance with the experiential realm, the realm of phenomena, form is animated with meaning. In this balance, architecture has both intellectual and physical intensity, with the potential to touch mind, eye, and soul (Holl 1994: 40).

For Holl, achieving "physical intensity" is a matter of creating constructions of space, materials and light that transform our day-to-day experience by sensitizing our consciousness to an authentic engagement in the immediacy of sensory experience – becoming as fully conscious as possible of our existence. This heightened state is focused through our "embodiment" – what Merleau-Ponty describes as the experience of our bodiliness in the world, *as lived,* free from any schism of mind from body. While we engage in inner mental phenomena as an inward awareness, we simultaneously engage in outward physical phenomena. As we can think deeply, so too are we capable of great engagement at the level of physical phenomena.

For Holl, "embodied" experience gives significance to acts of making. Workmanship, engagement in the purposeful formation of materials, gives precise properties to the perceptual structure of our physical surroundings. These properties endow the perception of objects with what Merleau-Ponty calls a "form giving" power that inherently relates to our embodiment by affording a way of knowing the world directly through its sensual nature (Merleau-Ponty 1981). This is the language of the world of objects. This language is within our comprehension; it is a fundamental understanding gained from the intimate knowledge we experience as we dwell within our bodies. Building design, then, is the materialization of the artifice of architecture in a *living* connection between mental and sensual content. For Holl, acts of making purposefully configure the world to realize the presence of sensory perception. The experiential immediacy in perception intensifies relations between our body immersed in its experience of the world and the interpretive world of mental concepts. One searches perception for questions – i.e., why has this been made and what are the motives behind it being made this way?

In the Addition to the Cranbrook Institute of Science in Michigan, Holl challenges occupants to engage in concepts of scientific thinking by immersing them in an environment of the senses. Two modes of construction help accomplish this. Daylight is manipulated in the building interior to express both its profound presence and its varying penetration over the course of the day. As the sun moves across the sky, no room is perceived the same way twice.

Skylights allow penetration in locations strategically positioned to alter the sensuality and geometry of architectural spaces. Light refracting skylight glazing distorts the entering sunlight into a living texture that effectively causes it to be perceived as the material substance

Figure 1
Photo by Stephen Temple

of the wall surface. This transfiguration of light into substance evokes the character of scientific research, centrally concerned as it is with such changes of state. The experiential connectivity of this realization is from senses to intellect – from phenomena to abstraction.

Wall and ceiling surfaces are constructed of plaster applied by hand in many thin layers, each with a differing color or fine textural character. Because they are applied by hand the depth of each thin layer varies slightly, giving the perception that various surfaces show though one another. Though there is little three-dimensional texture, the layered wall surface offers deep sensual interaction as thinly veiled layers interact with and vary color and light reflectance. The surface appears to change depending on one's proximity, developing a natural scaling coherence (Salingaros 1999). The wall has a hierarchically continuous sensual quality no matter from how far or close you see it. A painted wall, by contrast, ceases to look and feel different after moving only a few feet from it – it is only a colored skin, after all. Because visual perception requires constant motion, this plaster wall offers itself to our perception in living connection with our movements through perception and, thus, reciprocally realizes our embodiment in the *actual body of the building* – its illuminated space and surfaces.

There is an *interrelationship* between the way constructed things in the world are conceived, the way they have been made or produced, and the way they are received through perception. Attention to the nature of human perception can have great effect on the potential influence of man-made design on human feeling and thinking. In Holl's buildings, architectural experience is formed of an interdependence between the sensual particulars of physical phenomena and the generative concepts of *the maker* to simultaneously heighten perceptual phenomena in connection with developing meaning. For Steven Holl, architecture is as much a project of consciousness as a challenge of conceptualization, program and construction.

References

Holl, Steven. 1994. "Questions of Perception-Phenomenology of Architecture." In Steven Holl, Juhani Pallasmaa, Alberto Pérez-Gómez. *Questions of Perception-Phenomenology of Architecture.* Tokyo: *A+U Special Issue.*

Merleau-Ponty, Maurice. 1981. *Phenomenology of Perception.* London: Routledge & Kegan Paul.

Salingaros, Nikos A. 1999. "A Scientific Basis for Creating Architectural Forms." *Journal of Architectural and Planning Research*, 15(4): 283–93.

Landmark Destination: Jay Pritzker Pavilion

Joy Monice Malnar

Joy Monice Malnar, M.Arch, is an associate professor in the School of Architecture at the University of Illinois at Urbana-Champaign. She is the co-author of *Sensory Design* and *The Interior Dimension: A Theoretical Approach to Enclosed Space*. malnar@uiuc.edu

In Chicago, a city of landmark skyscrapers, the Jay Pritzker Pavilion serves as a new sort of landmark that brings us down to earth. Even though it stands 120 feet high – no mean height – the festive pavilion is dwarfed by its neighbors. These include the dignified 1,136- foot Aon Center that now serves as a backdrop to this centerpiece of Millennium Park. Chicagoans and tourists alike were drawn toward the unusual Pritzker Pavilion even in its early phases of construction. A common question asked by local residents and tourists alike was: "What is it?" The novelty of the beckoning structure indicated early on signs of its becoming a landmark destination.

The Pritzker Pavilion, designed by Frank Gehry, comprises a series of billowing curves of brushed stainless steel panels.[1] During the day it reflects the sun's passage, becoming a bright object that attracts our attention, and at night its theatrical, colored lighting serves as a beacon. The complex consists of two parts that, arguably, are not architecturally cohesive but do work together to provide a social function – that of gathering Chicagoans and tourists together. In fact, this complex functions like a small town gazebo of the past, but at a grander, urban scale. Thus the pavilion functions as both urban icon and socially interactive area, both on the stage and off. People-watching takes place under the monumental trellis system that gracefully sweeps outward from the stage and spreads over the 95,000-square-foot lawn. This square footage translates into a space two American football fields long and one wide. It includes 4,000 fixed seats and a lawn area that accommodates approximately 7,000 people, depending on whether they are just sitting on the grass or claiming a larger area with picnic blankets. The practical function of the trellis is to hold the thin cables of the sound system above the audience without blocking the view of the stage – but it also heightens the human connection of those gathered together, as well as providing a place where people can come to relax and daydream.

A touching passage in Alex Kotlowitz's book, *There Are No Children Here* describes a lush manicured lawn as "a small paradise … a refuge … a respite…" for a young boy living in one of Chicago's housing projects in the 1980s. It was a place "where nothing would interrupt his daydreaming…" as the "grass carpet offered a quiet resting place…" (Kotlowitz [1991] 1992: 143). People living in the suburbs typically take for granted the sensorial experience of lawns, an experience less common to urbanites. Along the western edge of Millennium Park lies a solid wall of historically significant buildings, which have been converting to condominiums in record numbers. According to a Brookings Institution report, in 2000 Chicago ranked number one nationwide in the proportion of downtown residences that were owner-occupied. Since then, another twenty-thousand housing units have been added to the downtown area. (Handley 2005). As residents move back to the inner city they are relieved to find just outside their front door a front lawn worthy of any prestigious suburb.

Suburban single-family home owners are trading in their lawn-mowers, but not the smell of cut grass, which is one of the odors most likely to bring on feelings of nostalgia and which fulfills a psychological need. (A 1991 survey by Dr Alan Hirsch of Chicago of scent-related feelings showed that young Chicagoans did not necessarily share the positive memories earlier generations associated with cut grass (Hirsch, 1992).) The Pritzker Great Lawn is set above the parking garage and back from the congested city streets; thus removed from the smells of exhaust and the sounds of traffic it becomes a green oasis.

While the pavilion can be seen from a distance by car or bus, it can only be approached on foot. At pedestrian speed the body is able to feel the sequence of spaces of transit from the dense grid of city sidewalks on the west – where there is little sense of the sky – to the great lawn where one's relationship to the blue sky and soft green grass is haptically felt. Seen from a distance the exuberant bandshell holds promise of a spatial experience, although upon arrival there is

Figure 1
Jay Pritzker Pavilion,
Millennium Park, Chicago.
© 2004 Joy Monice Malnar

a degree of disappointment. That is, it serves merely as a frame for a stage large enough to hold the full-sized Grant Park Orchestra with its 150-member chorus.

Fortunately, it is redeemed by the low-arched trellis that ultimately provides a feeling of spatial enclosure that embraces and gathers people on the lawn.

Grass typically provides a reduction in temperature from that experienced on city sidewalks and streets. Certain materials absorb more energy than others, so when the temperature of the city street feels like 100 degrees and the sidewalk feels like 90 degrees, the grass feels like only 80 degrees (Foster, 1994: 11). Even during the 2005 summer, one of the hottest in Chicago's history the crowds kept coming to the free concerts in numbers that surpassed projections. As the residents look out from their Michigan Avenue windows onto this lively outdoor family room, they are tempted to leave their air-conditioned rooms and experience the outdoors. Perhaps only in regions with four distinct seasons do people really know how to enjoy, celebrate and truly appreciate the sun, temperature and, yes, humidity of summer. While the high cost overruns of Millennium Park are being justified economically by the increased real estate values and larger numbers of tourists, the real value is in getting people outdoors and walking for the health benefits. The Pritzker flourish visually intrigues the eye, encouraging people to walk to a place where the state-of-the-art sound system, the first of its kind in the country, was designed to provide acoustics similar to those of an indoor concert hall. By distributing enhanced, perfectly timed, immersive sound equally over both the fixed seats and the lawn, everyone at this free venue can feel a part of the experience, an experience enhanced by the primal comfort of laying on the cool grass on a warm summer day. What may be the most interesting aspect of this building is that much of the money spent was for its iconic status, yet some of its most satisfactory aspects are those sensory characteristics we take for granted.

Notes

1. On a design this complicated it is difficult to credit all of the people involved in making the Pritzker Pavilion a success. Ed Uhlir, Mayor Richard Daley's project director for the park played a significant role. Also credit goes to Skidmore, Owings & Merrill for the master plan and engineering, Talaske Group, Oak Park for acoustics and audio consulting and the numerous contractors and tradesmen who were required to learn CATIA, the 3D computer-software system.

References

Foster, Ruth S. 1994. *Landscaping That Saves Energy and Dollars*. Old Saybrook, CT: Globe Pequot Press.

Handley, John. 2005. "Condo Stake Claim as 1st Choice for Downtown Chicago Living." *Chicago Tribune* (December 11), Business Section 5, p. 1.

Hirsch, Alan. 1992. "Scenting a Generation Gap." *Childrens' Environments*, 9(1): 13.

Kotlowitz, Alex. [1991] 1992. *There Are No Children Here: The Story of Two Boys Growing up in the Other American*. New York: Anchor Books, Doubleday.

Time (and Again): The Lurie Garden

David L. Hays

David L. Hays, M.Arch., Ph.D., is an assistant professor in the Department of Landscape Architecture at the University of Illinois at Urbana-Champaign. In 2004, he was the guest editor of *306090 07: Landscape within Architecture*. dlhays@uiuc.edu

In July 2000, the city of Chicago announced a competition for a "destination garden" to be situated in the southeast corner of the new Millennium Park. (Waldheim 2001). The scheme was to be horticulturally rich and visually engaging in all seasons, including winter. Furthermore, the position of the garden between the Great Lawn and access points to a vast parking garage below meant that it would be crossed by large numbers of pedestrians, particularly before and after performances in the nearby Pritzker Pavilion, for which the lawn would provide outdoor seating. Balancing those two conditions – a premium on complex planting design and the need to accommodate high-volume pedestrian traffic – became a principal challenge of the competition.

The winning entry – first called the Shoulder Garden and later renamed the Lurie Garden – featured two main planting areas (the so-called Light and Dark Plates) separated by a "seam" (a broad wooden footbridge over a channel of water). On the north and west sides of the garden, a colossal hedge (known as the Shoulder Hedge) served as a backdrop for views within the garden while isolating the space from the rest of the park.

David L. Hays

Figure 1
Lurie Garden,
Millennium Park, Chicago.
© 2004 David L. Hays

The design was produced through a collaboration between three parties: the Seattle-based landscape architecture office, Gustafson Guthrie Nichol; the Dutch plantsman, Piet Oudolf and the Los Angeles-based set and costume designer, Robert Israel. Israel's involvement alone reveals much about how the garden was conceived and meant to be experienced. The Millennium Park is primarily a venue for tourists and urban residents seeking entertainment, usually with cameras in hand. Israel works mainly for opera, in which a principal challenge is to relate stationary or slow-moving figures to large-scale settings. In keeping with those concerns, the Lurie Garden was designed as a set piece against which to visualize (and photograph) the human figure and through which to relate visitors to an idealized image of the city, its skyline. In such a theatrical approach to urban space making, vision is the critical sensory concern.

When installed, the Lurie Garden included something not seen in the competition drawings – signs asking visitors to stay on paths and keep out of planted areas. Those signs were intended to be subtle, yet they are highly distracting and make one wonder if touch could have been addressed differently. Ironically, the space in the Millennium Park most varied in textures is the one where touch is forbidden. In contrast, the nearby Cloud Gate – a massive, seemingly seamless bubble of polished steel – manipulates sight in a way that elicits and rewards touch. Its convex curvatures distort vision such that people have difficulty locating themselves within its reflections. Visitors impulsively approach the Cloud Gate in search of their own images. Many eventually touch its surface, confirming its materiality while finding and making contact with their own reflections. In the

Lurie Garden, touch is restricted, but at the Cloud Gate, touch is orienting and affirming.

Effective sensory design sometimes involves the suppression of one sense in favor of another. In the case of the Lurie Garden, could the scheme have been implemented without resorting to signs? For example, could the plants themselves have communicated to visitors that they should not be touched? Adjacent to the Millennium Park, in Dan Kiley's south garden at the Art Institute, a canopy of hawthorn trees with daunting spikes makes pedestrians keep their distance while giving an exaggerated sense of shelter to those seated beneath. As it happens, the office of Dan Kiley was also a finalist in the Millennium Garden competition. In its proposal, the central walkway was lined with small cockspur thorn trees garnished with menacing spikes. As in the south garden at the Art Institute, haptic experience is evoked without being engaged.

Could the Lurie Garden have been made differently, balancing the visual and the haptic? Gilles Clément's *jardin en mouvement* (garden in motion) in the Parc André-Citroën, Paris, is situated along the main circulation axis yet allows visitors immediate, immersive contact with vegetation. In contrast, the plantings in the Lurie Garden are "staged" on plates that tip up towards the west, as foregrounds to the skyline along Michigan Avenue. The beds are framed in a way that makes them seem precious, even sacrosanct. Even so, the design could have engaged visitors immersively in the sectional condition of the site: a soil plate (maximum depth forty-eight inches) over a three-story parking garage, in turn over train tracks.

According to Oudolf, one objective of the Lurie Garden is "to tell city people what they are missing in the countryside." (Freeman 2004: 103). In horticultural terms, that claim is absurd, even as it invokes a tradition of the urban public park as *rus in urbe* (the country in the city). Some of the literature surrounding the Lurie Garden relates it to the prairie (ironically, not a type of landscape ever found on this specific site) or to an idealized regional landscape. Yet, the plant list posted on the Millennium Park's website (as of November 2005) names 128 perennials, grasses and sedges, and shrubs, only forty-seven of which are "native" – defined on the list as "native to North America." Prairies are renowned for their economy, especially their ability to withstand water shortages. The plantings in the Lurie Garden are maintained with support from a ten-million-dollar endowment. That is sustainable design in fiscal terms, not natural ones.

What "city people" (i.e., those able to visit regularly) can gain from the Lurie Garden is a sense of natural time. Other features of the Millennium Park such as the Cloud Gate and the Crown Fountain ideally persist as installed, but the Lurie Garden is internally affected by seasonal and annual change. The Light and Dark Plates register time and can be read visually as a sort of calendar. Plant specialists should be able to interpret them with precision; others will witness change through repeat visits. To that end, the situation of the Lurie

Garden along a major pedestrian route will help foster appreciation of the very elements to which such exposure is ostensibly antagonistic. One-time visitors (e.g., tourists) will miss that dimension entirely.

References

Freeman, Allen, 2004. "Fair Game on Lake Michigan." *Landscape Architecture* 94 (11): 94–105.

Waldheim, Charles (ed.). 2001. *Constructed Ground: The Millennium Garden Design Competition*. Urbana, IL: University of Illinois Press.

BOOK AND JOURNAL REVIEWS

Mud, Sweat and Tears

Steve Redhead

Those Feet: A Sensual History of English Football, by David Winner, Bloomsbury: London, 2005, 288 pages. HB ISBN 9780747547389. £14.99

Professor of Sport and Media Cultures in the University of Brighton's Chelsea School, Steve Redhead is the author of twelve books, most recently *Paul Virilio: Theorist for an Accelerated Culture* and *The Paul Virilio Reader* (Edinburgh University Press, 2004) and the forthcoming *We Have Never been Postmodern*. Current research interests include mobile modernities and culture of cities
S.C.Redhead@brighton.ac.uk

The first book freelance journalist David Winner wrote was called *Brilliant Orange*, a study of the "Neurotic Genius of Dutch Football." In it he excavated the culture that produced what was once christened "Total Football" after the performance, tactics and style of the inspirational Holland team of the 1970s. It made his name as one of the so-called soccerati, the new football writers emerging in the 1990s who followed in the footsteps of Nick Hornby, like Winner a long-time, self-confessed Arsenal fan. The book sold widely and was well regarded by football fans and sport journalists. When his thoughts turned to Englishness and football culture there was almost inevitably born the present volume, *Those Feet*, a text that Winner admits can be regarded as the sequel. For those who think that the attenuated Blakean quotation is stunted and a little bizarre, the original title was even worse: courtesy of the Duke of Wellington, it was going to be called *By God They Frighten Me!*

What actually makes *Those Feet* of critical interest for us here is its subtitle: *A Sensual History of English Football*. A Sensual History of English Football would indeed be a fascinating contribution to the sensory formations project of which *The Senses and Society* journal forms part. It would reinvigorate studies of global sport and media cultures and help, as Marx says, to make the senses theoreticians in all kinds of ways. Unfortunately David Winners' book promises a great deal more than it delivers and a satisfactory "sensual history" of the national game in England will have to wait for another day. There are myriad cultural references contained in these pages from film, literature, social history, television, fanzines, newspapers, magazines and (even) academic books, and everyone from the Kinks and The Clash to Machiavelli and Carl Jung is name checked, but it remains an unsatisfactory mishmash. Early on in the book, Winner eagerly eschews "conventional history" and also "sociology," but what we get instead is an uncritical populist treatise without any great originality. "Jerusalem," the William Blake poem that Winner thinks "ought to be our national anthem" has become more pervasive in media sport events in England in recent years and was even played at cricket grounds before the start of Test Matches in the 2005 Ashes series against Australia to rally the home fans. But I couldn't hear the sound of it in this book. Moreover, I wanted to be able to smell "Those Feet" and reading the book I can't.

Winner occasionally springs a surprise. He is good on the "de-mudding" of football in England, for instance. As even the most casual observer of English Premiership football will know, the pitches on which top-class professional players ply their trade are as smooth as billiard tables throughout the season, a stark contrast to how the game played even as little as fifteen years ago. As Winner puts it (p. 183) "mud is now doomed, and elements of the English style are disappearing with it. Football of a speed and dainty technical excellence unimaginable in the past is now routinely played on the smoothest, firmest, best-quality grass pitches the game has ever seen." At this point, though, Winner becomes nostalgic, lamenting that there was "grace" in the ugly, muddy game, and noting that "as the mud vanishes, something of the old spirit of the game drains away too." The speed of football and its sensory implications is worth a chapter on its own, but in fact in Winner's book there is little analysis of the modern highly designed and engineered ball which swerves, at manufacturers' insistence, at stunning velocity like a predator drone, making goalkeepers fear just about any shot never mind the penalty. The speed of the sporting media and the speed of the game are integrally connected and serious study would have paid dividends yet Winner spends much of his time rehashing quotations about football and its history from either low or high cultural roots – here a Bill Shankly speech, there an E.M.Forster reference – without much end product. His first chapter, entitled "Sexy Football" a phrase earlier made famous by Ruud Gullitt, the great Dutch master, is a revisiting of the tenuous connections between masturbation and social purity discourses of the nineteenth century and the social history of football in England.

Overall, this book represents a missed opportunity to embark on sensual histories of sporting cultures. We should, nevertheless, be grateful to David Winner for at least signposting the way forward in his subtitle to *Those Feet*.

SENSORY FORMATIONS SERIES

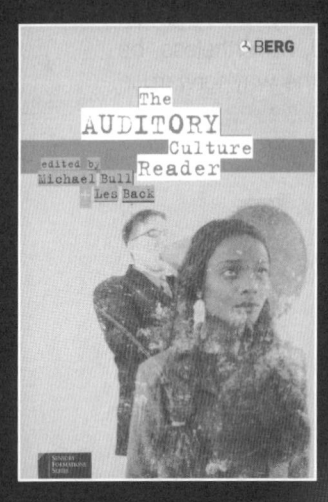

Edited by Michael Bull & Les Back
December 2003
HB 1 85973 613 0   £55.00 $99.95
PB 1 85973 618 1   £18.99 $32.95

Edited by David Howes
December 2004
HB 1 85973 858 3   £60.00 $99.95
PB 1 85973 863 X   £19.99 $29.95

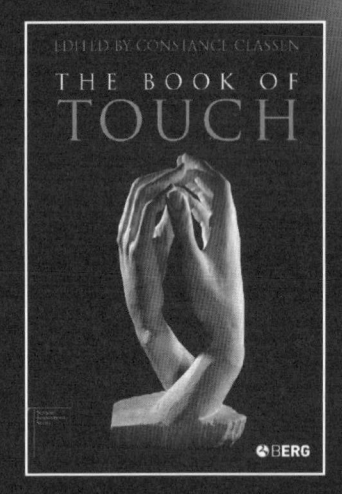

Edited by Constance Classen
July 2005
HB 1 84520 058 6   £55.00 $99.95
PB 1 84520 059 4   £19.99 $34.95

Edited by Carolyn Korsmeyer
August 2005
HB 1 84520 060 8   £55.00 $99.95
PB 1 84520 061 6   £19.99 $34.95

www.bergpublishers.com

Seeing Under the Skin

Anna-Louise Milne

The Senses of Modernism: Technology, Perception, and Aesthetics, by Sara Danius, Ithaca and London: Cornell University Press. 2002, 256 pages. PB 0-8014-8800-1.

Anna-Louise Milne is a lecturer in the French Department at the University of London Institute, Paris. She has written mainly on Jean Paulhan (most recently *The Extreme In-Between. Jean Paulhan's Place in the Twentieth Century*, Legenda 2006) and *The Nouvelle Revue Française*. She is currently preparing a work on pacifism and literary movements in the early twentieth century. anna-louise. milne@wanadoo.fr

Beginning with a chapter on the anti-technological bias of discourses on modernism, which explores a variety of articulations of the opposition between high art and mass-produced culture, and ending with an excursus via Hegelian idealism and the premises that modernism is modern because it makes the body the primary vehicle of aesthetic experience, Sara Danius's lively book narrates the progressive internalization of technologically generated modes of perception, arguing that modernism cannot be understood independently of the stresses and possibilities associated with the "second machine age."

The reader is invited to consider the extent to which new technologies, particularly those of photography and cinematography, transform the perceptual modes of three major exemplars of what Danius recognizes to be the amorphous notion of modernism, that is, Mann, Proust and Joyce. Highlighting the reliance of these "great" writers on mechanisms of popular culture is intended to collapse any distinction between high and low. Thus in the chapter on Mann, Danius argues convincingly that the new perceptions enabled by x-ray technology make other modes of knowledge seem arbitrary and ossified, particularly the social mores of bourgeois society and its medical discourse. *The Magic Mountain* is shown to bring conflicting visual regimes to play against one another, even while it attempts to present the novel as the form where lyric, medical and technological sensibilities can co-exist. The totalizing humanist project struggles to stabilize the drive to know sparked off by the mechanical eye of the x-ray that can see the death of the subject, and the Hegelian elevation to the aesthetic that is inscribed in the novel is undercut by a preoccupation with human finitude brought into focus by technological apparatus.

But Danius's narrative drive is more faltering in the chapter on Proust, and this shift in gear is masked by the strong teleological structure that she articulates to weld the parts of the book together. Bridging the gap between the quite specific and arresting experience of x-rays in *The Magic Mountain*, which opens the modernist phase, and the chapter on Joyce, in which reference to specific devices drops out almost altogether to leave an analysis of the autonomy of sensory perception in *Ulysses*, lies *Remembrance of Things Past*, a radically different object to either *The Magic Mountain* or *Ulysses*, and one to which Danius dedicates a considerably longer chapter. She sets Proust's traditional hierarchy of the arts and of perception against the numerous and crucial passages describing experiences made possible only by technologies of vision and speed. The chapter concludes that the premium Proust placed on seeing as the truth of experience, in the same tradition as Ruskin, Turner or Bergson, in fact operated by means of instruments that abstract, frame or fix human experience. Thus technoscientific possibilities of perception are shown to be increasingly incorporated by an author who, for all his nostalgia, is enthused by the new forms of aesthetic gratification. Consequently Proust's disparaging discourse on photography as a superficial art form is relativized, and the distinction between aesthetic autonomy and merely technological culture is undermined.

The problem with all this lies in the emphasis on the seeing for seeing sake, the term that enables a link between a concept of high-modernism and the increasing prevalence of technologically mediated experience. This suppresses the insistent quest for knowledge that runs throughout *Remembrance of Things Past*, the complex social and sexual initiation that fuels large sections of the novel. Visual prostheses play a vital role in this process, entering the text to mediate a particularly difficult process of discovery for the narrator. Danius analyses some of these key passages (the famous kiss of Albertine, Saint-Loup's fistfight) but she is content to note merely that technology is being tapped in the pursuit of "perceptual innocence," fulfilling the Ruskian ideal of rescuing the senses from the rationalizing patterns of habit, but only by means of abstracting devices. In this respect, the realization about Saint-Loup's sexuality generated by the vision of the fistfight, for example, is of the same order as the famous involuntary memory that supposedly generates the great extension of Proust's novel. This posits a unity and coherence to Proust's novel that Danius's own theoretical premises do much to resist, and arguably it closes down the significance of the very range of sensory mechanisms upon which Proust calls precisely by straining to emphasize the naturalization of photographic awareness.

It should be no surprise that Danius's attempt to articulate the technological and the modernist together comes somewhat adrift in the chapter on *Remembrance of Things Past* since this novel bears a much more complex relation to concepts of modernism than either *The Magic Mountain* or *Ulysses*. Yet what may seem like a failing in this tightly written book in fact hides a strength, for it raises the stakes of the critical investigation far beyond merely correcting the antitechnological bias in modernist discourse, and invites a much broader exploration of technology's constitutive role in experience.

JOURNAL OF THE SOCIETY FOR VISUAL ANTHROPOLOGY

Visual Anthropology Review

As the journal of the Society for Visual Anthropology, *Visual Anthropology Review* promotes the discussion of visual studies, broadly conceived. Within its breadth, visual anthropology includes both the study of visual aspects of human behavior and the use of visual media in anthropological research, representation and teaching. The journal welcomes articles, reviews and commentary on the use of multimedia, still photography, film, video and non-camera generated images, as well as on visual ideologies, indigenous media, applied visual anthropology, art, dance, gesture, sign language, human movement, museology, architecture and material culture.

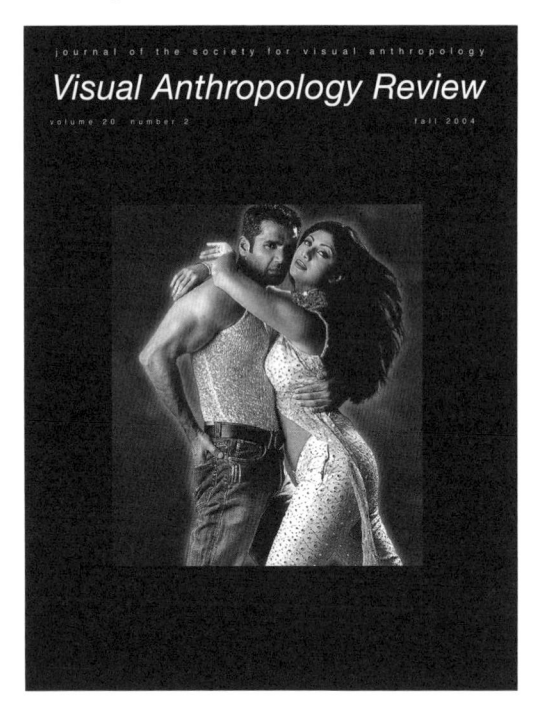

Visual Anthropology Review
http://etext.virginia.edu/VAR/

Changing Senses Across Cultures

Judith Okely

"The Senses," *Etnofoor* 18(1) 2005. Guest editors Regina Bendix and Donald Brenneis. Anthropological-Sociological Centre, Spinhuis, Oudezijds Achterburgwal 185, 1012 DK Amsterdam. ISBN 3-8258-9108-9 / ISSN 09215158. Single journal edition €12.00.

Judith Okely is Emeritus Professor of Anthropology, Hull University and Deputy Director of IGS, Queen Elizabeth House, Oxford University. Her publications include The *Traveller-Gypsies* (1983), *Simone de Beauvoir* (1986), *Anthropology and Autobiography* (1992), *Own or Other Culture* (1996) and articles in *Ethnos* (2001), *Journal of Media Practice* (2003) and *The Sociological Review* (2005).
J.M.Okely@hull.ac.uk

The privileging of detachment was once rife in approaches to fieldwork. Anthropologists rarely disclosed their own bodily experiences or those of their "informants." Now, increasingly, the body and the senses are being integrated into theories and practice. This *Etnofoor* special journal issue, devoted to the senses, is a case in point. It offers a cornucopia of possibilities, enchantments and pain.

Across human bodies there are divisions and solidarities, differences and resonances. Many anthropologists, released from pseudo-scientific encasement, are sensitized to different ways of knowing beyond notebook inscriptions, cerebral interviews and surveillance. The articles collected here interrogate inhibitions or omissions of the senses with examples from England, China, Ecuador, Scotland, Australia, Japan and Uganda.

In her introduction, Bendix advocates "sensory holism in the field" rather than treating the senses as a subdiscipline. We can return to Proust. She also hints at knowledge through pain and violence. Relations with the environment may be peaceful or catastrophic. So, I suggest, sensory knowledge is not merely the "touchy-feely" approach that cerebral critics denigrate. But how ethnographers acquire it has hardly been discussed.

Bendix does not entirely blame the bias towards logocentric and ocularcentric ethnographic approaches for the neglect of the full range of the senses. Sensory paucity may be attributable to fieldwork technologies that have impeded the anthropologist from recognizing his or her own body as a primary instrument. It is disconcerting that fieldwork practice for some was reduced to the interventionist interlocutor/scribe. However, Bendix still tends to present the body merely as a means to augment ethnographic depth. This again risks sidelining the use of the senses.

In the early 1980s there were few anthropology methods books. Paradoxically, the neophyte was free to take participant observation literally as a form of social and bodily engagement not just as co-residence and reportage. From my dialogs with anthropologists who conducted fieldwork from the 1970s it is apparent that many were indeed uncontaminated by instrumentalist pedagogies. They learned through their bodies and shared experience, not simply through interrogations. The main difference between their texts and those here is that the former did not expound on *how* they acquired that knowledge, nor have they always written specifically about others' sensory knowledge.

Many *Etnofoor* contributors reveal how they learned and interpreted sensual knowledge in fieldwork. Marvin attended English fox hunts (as foot follower or on horseback?) He evokes the multi-sensory practice and is not concerned here with meaning but with "how it is to hunt." Hunting for pleasure contrasts with instrumental hunting for food. The huntsmen do not creep up on the animal but, through the medium of dogs, deliberately disturb the fox and provoke the chase. The article evokes the huntsmen's sensual experiences and the use of dogs to scent the othered animal. However, the reader may not be able to empathize with the terrorizing conquest where sensory pleasure derives from an animal's pain.

Lund reiterates a growing awareness that there are different forms of vision, an eye that observes but also reflects. Elsewhere (*Ethnos* 2001), I have distinguished "looking" from "seeing" and suggested links between bodily labor, views of the worked landscape and the taste of its produce among Normandy farmers. The claim that Western epistemology has privileged only one form of vision is unraveling. Lund draws on her own embodied experience to examine mountain walking in Scotland. There are limitations inherent in the observing eye in contrast to the "touching eye." The walker shifts from focusing on the ground to looking into the distance. Bodily sensation is crucial; especially the way the feet touch the ground. Her study of leisure walkers might address class and identity. Gamekeepers and poachers will have different views and movement styles in those locations.

In contrast, Walmsley presents vital links between sensory experience, place and ethnicity in black, indigenous or mestizo culture in Ecuador. In a subtle analysis, using the notion of "emplacement," she demonstrates interconnections between the senses and habitus. Selective cuisines express ethnic boundaries between the othered blacks and Hispanic peoples. Taste and smell are molded through socialization and open to changes. The ethnography accommodates migration and movements through varying localities. Cuisine identified with "home" can be transformed by incomers, mixed-race families and hybrid offspring. Two articles present preliminary explorations of, for example, fragrance in Japan (Moeran) and a linguistic approach to perception of signs in Southern Uganda (Orlove and Kabugo).

A major contribution is what Young has presented as "cultural synaesthesia" among the Pitjantjaara people in the Western Desert of Australia. Young considers the people's emphasis on color. She brilliantly expounds the way people make correspondences between color and odor – namely the sight of greenness and the smell of the land after prolonged rain brings immediate germination and new growth. The ethnography links these senses to taste, ingestion and bodies in landscapes. Her critical outline of Western psychology's study of synesthesia exposes the ethnocentric assumption that this phenomenon is a-social, unlearnt and confined to the individual, disembodied brain. Instead, Young demonstrates the cultural specificity and the plasticity of such merging of senses. This is a superb example of anthropology's critique of reductionist debates about human universals.

Sensory knowledge is not all pleasure. Hsu analyses pain not from afar but through consenting "participant experience" of acupuncture in China. Acute pain infliction is considered therapeutic and connects patient and healer. It can be a necessary ingredient in both healing and life-cycle events. Acute pain she differentiates from chronic pain; the latter leads to isolation. Her discussion confronts a Western medical practice that minimizes pain and encourages fragmentation and loss of (Durkheimian?) social cohesion.

This volume demonstrates the need for detailed cross-cultural studies of sensory knowledge. Humans have common bodily aspects that are sensed differently through cultural practices. Gender, "race" and identity through place are affirmed through sensory being and doing. Often the anthropologist can only become sensitized to cultural specificities, beyond the cerebral, through his or her own malleable and permeable body. The challenge is how to recreate these insights, tastes, sounds or touchings on paper, something that this volume works in novel ways to achieve.

References
Okely, J. 2001. "Visualism and Landscape: Looking and Seeing in Normandy." *Ethnos*, 66(1): 99–120.

EXHIBITION REVIEWS

The Urban Sensorium

Sense of the City/Sensations Urbaines, curated by Mirko Zardini, at the Canadian Centre for Architecture, Montreal, October 26, 2005 to September 10, 2006.
Website: www.cca.qc.ca

Making Sense of the City
Alan Nash

Alan Nash (Ph.D. Cambridge) is Chair and associate professor in the Department of Geography, Planning and Environment at Concordia University in Montreal. From 2002 to 2005 he served as Secretary-Treasurer of the Canadian Association of Geographers. His research activities and academic publications deal with cultural geography and Canadian immigration policies.
nash@vax2.concordia.ca

This wonderful exhibition provides a fascinating introduction to the new realms of urban existence currently being discovered by researchers of the senses. And, rather like the senses that are its focus, it is an exhibition that stimulates and makes us curious in equal measure.

Divided into five sections (corresponding to broadly accepted notions regarding the number of senses we have), the exhibition presents ways in which sight, smell, sound, touch and perception of temperature are experienced as part of our everyday lives in the city.

After an introduction, in which our senses are contextualized within the much wider realm of animal and insect senses, the visitor to the exhibition proceeds (if she or he turns right – which, I am told, most museum visitors do) to encounter the first realm: that of sight. This is presented by an examination of the effects of night on the city. For example, do street lights cut down violence? Jane Jacobs is quoted as saying they don't. Her views are largely ignored, however, by utility corporations, planners and architects who harp on the value of urban electrification. Light fetishism of this sort makes us miss a great deal, as some amazing photographs of buildings at night suggest. Darkness forces us to experience the city in new ways and to open up unused parts of our perception to the full range of urban experience. This finding is an obvious one to the blind, and this part of the exhibition also includes Braille and tactile city maps as a way of promoting wider reflection on this issue.

The second set of displays, the "seasonal city," is concerned with our perception of temperature and deals (not surprisingly for Montreal in the winter) with ice, snow and cold. Photographs of skaters and ice palaces contrast with video clips of snow removal to show that the challenges of winter in an urban milieu are balanced by the joy of different recreational activities. Interestingly, the way in which snow dampens noise levels and increases the reflection of city lights also nicely illustrates how a range of our senses, rather than only one, can be engaged by the various phenomena of the urban "sensorium."

Temperature is followed by sound, a portion of the exhibition that relies mainly on the work of Canadian composer, R. Murray Schafer. Over a number of years now, he has endeavored to record the sounds of the city, and visitors can compare his 1973 Vancouver "soundscape" with those of a sample of other cities. This work is supplemented by researchers who have mapped the decibel levels across Zurich, and Minneapolis-St Paul. It very much seems that noise levels are increasing and have become a pervasive part of modern urban existence. It also seems that we don't mind – at least, the current use of the iPod to carry noise around with us seems to suggest this (although "sound" and "noise" are very much value judgments, as the exhibition makes clear).

The fourth part of the exhibition deals with asphalt as an example of how the surfaces of the city are covered. Once dusty and rugged boardwalks and rutted muddy roads are now smoothed over and covered with blacktop to create an anodyne world of neat parking lots (nicely parodied in some recent urban projects, as photos exhibited here indicate).

The final stop on the sensorial tour presents the world of smell. The visitor is invited to open vials in order to sniff various odors (such as bread, grass and rain) and to consider how air conditioning has dulled our experience of the atmosphere. By way of contrast, a view of an Italian hotel seemingly built of walls of flowers offers a prospect of some amazing new realm of experience.

What that new realm might be, we can only guess, but some working conclusions can certainly be gleaned from the exhibition, and from some of its subtexts. First, it very much appears that our recent urban experience has been one that has been almost completely shaped and conditioned by our sense of sight. For example, our cities and houses may be "planned," but attention is given mainly

Exhibition Review

to the visual aesthetics of a design. The feel of a surface, the sound emitted by its materials, or the smell of its activities are relegated to the backburner. It seems to me to be entirely symptomatic of this approach that the very disciplines of geography, urban planning and architectural studies have become almost entirely visual activities.

Why have we lost our senses? Clues provided by the exhibition clearly point to the processes of modernization, and to the passion we have to divorce ourselves from nature. This desire (itself perhaps a result of an Enlightenment separation between humans and the rest of nature) is one that modern technologies have only encouraged us to develop – often to our considerable disadvantage. Photos of

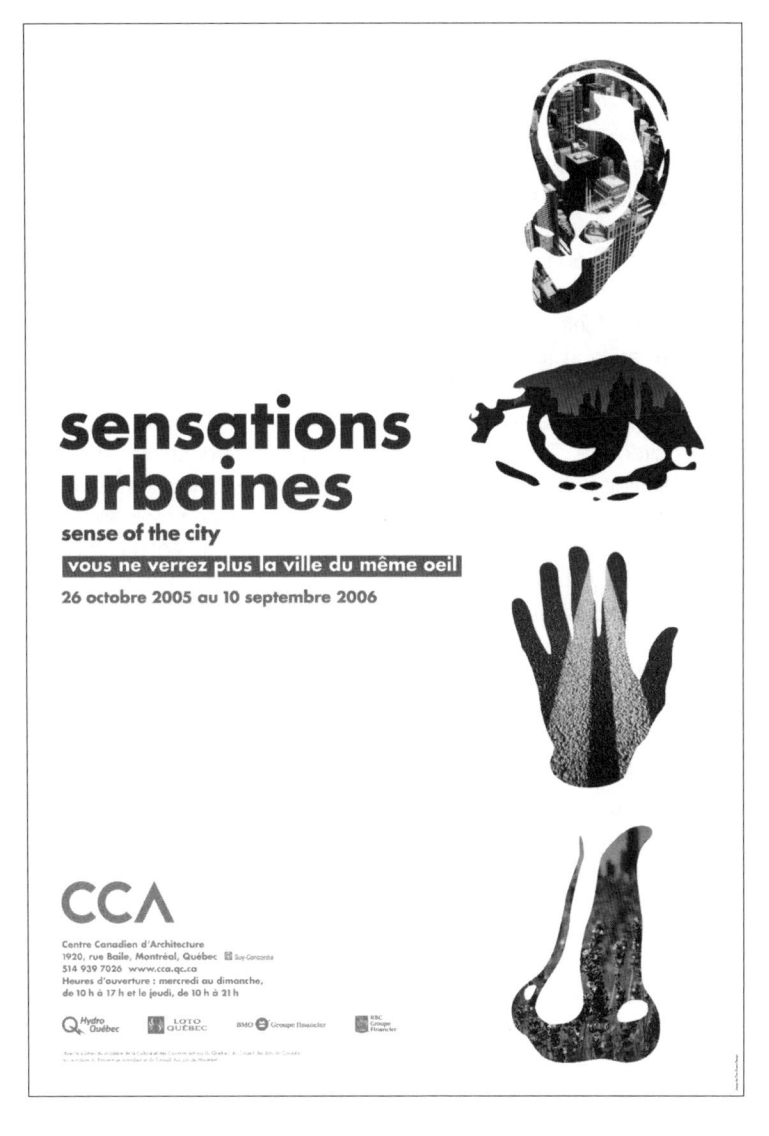

Poster for the exhibition
Sense of the City
© Centre Canadien
d'Architecture/Canadian
Centre for Architecture,
Montréal

Exhibition Review

"bubbles" erected over entire cities are emblematic of this trend – we want to be sealed off from the rough edges of the world and to live in an urban cocoon. Snow clearance provides another example – cities like Montreal now clear snow throughout the winter so that everyone can get to work as usual. But why should we expect this? Why do we try to use technology to "smooth away" an entire season? What hubris is this?

But maybe technology isn't all that bad? Certainly, a third and final reflection on this exhibition is that, exciting as it was, we probably don't want to go back to a Dickensian world of urban life. Unnavigable streets piled high with snow in the winter are one thing, but streets covered with horse dung are a hygiene risk. Smog may be very evocative of Sherlock Holmes, but to an asthmatic it can be life-threatening. Modernity and health concerns have therefore combined to produce an erosion of the senses in the re-shaping of our urban experience, but it is probably only a sentimentalist who would wish to restore that picture.

However this picture is ultimately viewed, the rediscovery of the world of the senses is an exciting story, and it is one that this exhibition expertly tells. Neither overly academic nor annoyingly superficial, it is an exhibition that wears its learning lightly and leaves us with a host of challenging questions. To have done this in such a relatively small space is both a tribute to the exhibition curators and to the power of the topic itself – for it is one that is both very simple and deeply transformative at the same time. The same comments apply to the book that accompanies the exhibition (Mirko Zardini (ed.), *Sense of the City: An Alternate Approach to Urbanism*: The Canadian Centre for Architecture, 2005). It usefully reproduces everything shown in the exhibition itself, and includes a series of specially-commissioned essays that will be welcomed by those who have had their appetites whetted by the exhibition and want to know more. Most of us probably give little thought to how we sense the city, but those who have seen this exhibition will never experience it in the same way again.

Prière de ne pas toucher
Michael Carroll

Michael Carroll is a designer based in Montreal where he is an adjunct professor of architecture at McGill University. He is a recipient of Canada's 2004 Prix de Rome in Architecture and in 2005 traveled extensively in Italy, Japan and the Netherlands as part of his research in urban interstitial interventions. m_carroll@sympatico.ca

The exhibition *Sense of the City*, curated by CCA director Mirko Zardini, opened at the Canadian Centre for Architecture in the Fall 2005 and closes in September 2006. The exhibition proposes a sensorial urbanism that challenges traditional urban design practices that privilege vision over the other senses, thus editing out a whole spectrum of experiences and limiting both the designer's and citizen's holistic sense of the city.

Sense of the City, designed by the architects of Atelier In Situ and the graphic designers of Orange Tango, starts with an elongated and slightly tapered, blacked-out corridor that features residual sounds of the city – a kind of visual palette cleanser for what's ahead. There is lots of text on the walls throughout the exhibit and one of the first snippets is the self-critical question: "Could you make a museum exhibit for the way of life in your city or town?" Well, yes and possibly no. However, *Sense of the City* promises to offer abundant clues for all those ambitious do-it-yourselfers.

The subdued "welcome room" of the exhibit offers graphic punch with large silhouettes of critters with advanced sensorial capabilities compared to us limited humans. Just think how a giant rat with a hearing range between 1,000 and 40,000 Hz, or an ant that can detect miniscule earth movements, experiences the world – we can only respond by becoming more aware of our own animalistic selves – hopefully encompassing senses well beyond the traditional Aristotelian five of sight, taste, touch, smell and hearing.

Heading to the right, clockwise around the central front room, the remaining five rooms of the CCA have been divided up to tackle and ponder the contemporary aspects of the post-industrial city. Each room, *nocturnal city*, *seasonal city*, *sounds of the city*, *surface of the city* and *air of the city*, is aligned, more or less, with one or two of the five senses with the exception of taste.

Nocturnal city focuses on sight by limiting it. Colonized by the eye, the darkness of night becomes a safer place – as Jane Jacobs has pointed out, eyes are more important than light when it comes to safety. Whether visually impaired or not, museum patrons are asked to touch an audio tactile guide of the city of Bologna, a Braille map of New York's subway system and maybe even the rubberized surface of the black plinth on which these items are displayed. *Seasonal city* focuses on snow and ice and their possibly numbing effects as we deny their existence in most of our Nordic cities. Images of the pavilions designed for *The Snow Show* held in 2004 in Lapland and sepia pictures of Montreal ice palaces, of around the late nineteenth century, offer ideas on how to embrace ice as a way of building a more festive future. *Sounds of the city* is an insular room furnished with low, rounded ottomans and headphones that conveys, among other things, Vancouver/New York soundscapes. It also features a drawer filled with lavender, an olfactory cue for the design of a two-meter-high acoustic wall along a highway in France generously covered with lavender. *Surface of the city* focuses on asphalt and visitors are encouraged to touch a tray of polymer modified asphalt or (despite the Duchampian *prière de ne pas toucher*) a crumbling hunk of asphalt. As well, asphalt's smooth ubiquitous character and its aesthetic potential are considered in a series of contemporary design projects, juxtaposing some earlier images of dirt and cobblestone streets also displayed in the room. *Air of the city* explores the homogenizing effect of air conditioners and is dominated by Ivan Ilich's pronouncement: "Increasingly the whole world has come to smell alike…" Exhibits include images and documentation of Gordon Matta-Clark's *Fresh Air Cart* performance piece and his photograph, *Pipes*, taken in 1971, that is cunningly displayed within the cavity of the museum's wall. Once again we are encouraged to engage our

Exhibition Review

senses by smelling tall laboratory beakers mounted on a plinth and filled with such simulated smells as subway detergent, garbage or grass.

As an exhibition, *Sense of the City* does offer a whiff of possible futures of a sensorial urbanism. Considerable academic weight is made with the addition of the exhibition's lecture series, special events and most importantly the catalog, *Sense of the City: An Alternative Approach to Urbanism*, published by the CCA and Lars Müller Publishers that features such delicious titles as: "The Idea of Winterness: Embracing Ice and Snow," "The Deodorized City: Battling Urban Stench in the Nineteenth Century" and "Sensory Stirrings."

Sense of the City is an ambitious project with real possibilities to shift the minds of urban planners, architects and artists as they consider the past, the present and the future of our increasingly urbanized environments. However, *Sense of the City*, despite it good intentions, falls short of its full potential because it is too tasteful, too polite and too intellectual to deal with the hugely divergent and possibly offensive nature of our cities. Museums do not like things to be messy or fuzzy – however, fortunately for us, cities are both. Cities are interesting because of the collision between very different things: the permanent and the temporal, the tasteful and the garish, the sacred and the profane. How can we program or propagate the accidental – without short circuiting it? How can an exhibition capture within the confines of the museum, an immersive urban atmosphere with all its multisensory complexity? Maybe a sensorial urbanism cannot be dissected – it can only exist within the space of contamination. Maybe somewhere between this sound, that smell and a multitude of other factors exists the essence of what is New York, Paris or New Delhi – forever elusive and mysterious, very far from the white rooms of any museum. As an alternative scenario, the street itself might be sensorial urbanism's next stop with all its profound fecundity with no *prière de ne pas toucher* in sight.